Printed in Cusco, Peru by CBC, 2003

ISBN: 0-9741806-0-2

www.cuscotales.com

Publishing
USA

Hecho el Depósito legal 0801012003-2082

ACKNOWLEDGEMENTS

Writing something on such a personal level as this is like being nude on a bus. Everybody's going to look at you, and depending upon their reaction, you'll either put your clothes on and get off at the next stop or hang in there buck-naked and start dancing.

The encouragement I got from those of you who accepted my email from Cusco kept me dancing. Thanks to Al Nisbet, Andrea Johnson, Bob & Dawn Rehm, Bill Rehm, Don Daniel, Colleen Nystedt, Cynthia Munzer, Kurt Bennett, Gary Glaze, Cassie Nisbet, Dave Cooper, Liz Nisbet, Drew and Jane Daniels, Eric Warner, Bob Fries, Hope Zaccagni, Horacio Ocampo, Jan Siegelman, Judy Kaplan, Kit Rosenlund, Linda Chelgren, Ed Gately, Bill Cooper, Lola McMillan, Marty Borko, Rene Hasler, Nancy Rapoport, Phillip Franchini, Scott Wyant, Tony & Marie Pope, Sharron Hasler, Tom & Lisa Hebenstreit, Wayne & Tina Preston, Vincent Pavis, Hope Calabrese, Chris Brough, Emilie Brough, Jim Larson, Mark and Elizabeth Ean, Dickie Lapalm, Leslie Betts and Lee & Magui Nolan.

Thanks also to those locals in Cusco who have made me feel comfortable here: Wilfredo, Carlos, Joel, Mario, Yahira, Wilson, Fritz, Leo, Lili, Yony, Marisol, Carina, Flore, Lucho, Yheni, Gladis, Jane, Carlos, Tito, Talo, Lance, Kike, Gladis, Jorge, David, Edward, Juan Ramon, Raul, Mauricio, Carolina, Luis, Yuri, Walquer, Yasmine, Anna, Jeroen, Tati, Tino, all the folks at Amaru Hostal, and of course, to Jeff, Charlie, Betty and Gary.

Thanks to Rosa Inez Figueroa Espinosa, who surprised me with her in-depth knowledge of printing and saved me from making the kind of mistakes I usually make when getting myself into an unfamiliar enterprise.

And special thanks to my former student, now teacher, Patrick Molloy. This would not have happened without you, my dear friend. Your support and advice have been invaluable.

Most of the people and places in these tales are real or at least were real when the tales were written. Because of my enthusiasm, it may appear that this book is a put-up job… that the city of Cusco and the establishments mentioned herein were somehow involved financially with the project. This is not the case, and a reading of the book will make that abundantly clear.

<u>No</u> chamber of commerce would sanction these stories.

There are many fine bars and restaurants in Cusco. I happened to land at those that are mentioned in these tales, and once I find a place I like, I tend to stick with it. I suggest that you find *your* places in Cusco. It might be different than mine.

<u>Experimentalo tu mismo</u>
(Find it for yourself)

This is for you,

My most amazing girls

Cass & Liz

Cusco Tales

by

Richard Nisbet

INDEX

CUSCO, PERU

Plaza de Armas

Cusco is not just a town, it is a place of God and man-made beauty. It is a crossroads, an experience. It is even a time machine of sorts. If you don't know Cusco, you're missing something. There's no other place like it. Ask anyone who's been there. It is the oldest inhabited city in the Western Hemisphere. They now call it "The archaeological capital of America." In Inca times they called Cusco "The Navel of the World."

It is spelled variously: Cusco, Cuzco, Qosqo. It is located in the Peruvian Andes, 13 degrees South of the Equator and depending upon where you're standing in the city, its elevation is around 10,000 to 12,000 feet above sea level. It's way up there. Some come from Lima on a bus. The trip takes up to 24 hours and traverses treacherous roads that edge precipitous drop-offs. But most tourists leave Lima on a one-hour flight that climbs over the snow-capped mountains of the Andes and drops into Cusco after making a hairpin turn, then threading its way between the mountain peaks that horseshoe around the city. Disembarking from the pressurized cabin of the plane, one is first greeted by a burning sensation in the lungs. To me it is pleasant, invigorating, promising. It means I'm back in my favorite town.

Cusco's population is somewhere around 300,000. But population figures give you no idea of what the city is like. On a busy day, the historic center of Cusco is a hubbub of activity rivaling that of New York's Fifth Avenue. Within a few blocks are scores of restaurants, bars, discos, shops and travel agencies. There is an astonishing number of internet *cabinas*, which all seem to be constantly and fully occupied with travelers and locals connecting with friends and the world at large. On first glance, central Cusco has the look of a typical Spanish colonial city. Most of the central plaza, the *Plaza de Armas*, has a perimeter of arched colonnades topped with ornately carved second-floor balconies. But if you take a closer look at the lower levels of the buildings, you see here and there remnants of the extraordinary stoneworks of the Incas, those few that were not totally destroyed by the Spanish when they devastated this vast and proud land in the mid 1500's.

Cusco was the center of a mighty empire that ranged along the

Andes cordillera from the interior of Colombia down to the Maule River in Chile. It was far and away the greatest empire of the pre-colonial new world. It was a civilization that rivaled in extent and effective governance of that of the Romans at the height of their expansion.

Cusco is a magnet for tourists who are not your typical upwardly mobile wonderbread vacationers. They come especially from Australia, New Zealand, Canada and Europe. Americans are in the minority. I surmise that this is because citizens of the United States of America are not so accustomed to world travel as much of the rest of the world, and when they do travel, Europe or the Middle East usually comes first. South America is low on the list.

The travelers I encounter in Cusco are usually a more adventurous sort. I do not include those who come here under the protection of packaged tours, who are herded from bus to ruin to cathedral and offered canned explanations, which are, more often than not, a collection of half-truths about the culture. I also do not speak of those who come here because of a belief that the messiah will land at Machu Picchu in a spaceship and transport them to a safe haven just as this world comes to an end.

I speak more of those who come alone, or with a companion, or with friends they've met along the path of their travels. Most of them come with limited finances, often porting only backpacks, often exploring the entire South American continent and making brief stops at this or that reputedly interesting town or ruin.

Sooner or later these intrepid travelers will come to Cusco. Sometimes they are here because this is the first stop on your way to hike the Inca trail or to make a brief visit to Machu Picchu.

But Cusco itself is a cultural and architectural jewel that warrants immersion.

One of my favorite pubs lies atop the remains of the Aclahuasi, the huge building that housed the king's chosen women. It is made of perfectly cut stones and it housed several thousand females whose sole purpose was to cater to the needs of the Inca, the Son of the Sun. The most beautiful of the women were his concubines. Others toiled daily to brew Chicha, the maize-based beer of the Andes, or to weave garments of Alpaca, Vicuna and Gold for the Inca. The latter was an interminable task, for the Inca wore his clothes for only one day. After that they were incinerated. No recycling, no hand-me-downs. The Inca, the king, was an absolute monarch that made most other monarchs in the history of mankind seem weak by comparison. When the Inca spat, one of his women was there to catch it in her hand so that the monarch's sputum might not touch the ground.

Cusco is like a village. If you lodge in the historic center of town, as I do, you can easily walk to the source of just about any of your needs. And if you don't want to walk, you can get a cab for 60 cents in the daytime or 90 cents at night.

The town is like a village, but it is a fascinating, global village. The continuous traffic of short to long-term visitors offers a vast perspective on the peoples of our planet. They are, by and large, curious, unconventional and ready for action.

Most of the local people, at least those not thieves are gentle and respectful. The young, with their coppery skin, their regal noses and hair the blackest of black, can be exceptionally beautiful. They tend to be shorter than average and the girls have adopted as fashion what might elsewhere be called elevator shoes... shoes of not only high heels, but also high soles. (I am reminded of the very short King Louis XIV, another Sun King, who did the same, only to have this height advantage trumped when all the court followed suit and adopted high heels.) The local girls, the *Cusqueñas*, tend to favor a clothing style that was popular in the US in the early 70's: tight-waisted leather jackets and bell bottom jeans. Lately a marijuana leaf has become a design motif. Recently I saw a pair of jeans on a girl with a large cannabis leaf centered on her crotch. A local friend who is a student at the university tells me that the older people have no idea that it is the leaf of the demon weed.

There are thieves here as there are all over the world. But the thieves here rarely use weapons, and almost never firearms. They may pick your pocket. They may slit your backpack or camera strap to rip you off. They may have an accomplice spit on you or throw a water bomb on you so that they can rush in and take advantage of your confusion. If they see you wandering a deserted street late at night, obviously drunk, they may cold-cock you to lift your wallet and jacket. But generally they don't kill and they don't maim. As thieves go, they are a refreshing lot. My experience is that if you exercise reasonable caution, you'll be okay here. I have never been mugged. Knock knock.

Cusco lies in the cul de sac of a valley. It is surrounded on three sides by mountains. In the rainy season, those mountains are several shades of green, some of it neon-intense. The houses are mostly of a deep reddish brown adobe. They are roofed with lighter reddish brown terra cotta tiles. The effect of the various greens and reds is more than pleasing. It is as inspiring as a Vermeer.

The weather in Cusco is benign. It never freezes, never even snows, never gets sticky hot, or even dry hot. It varies from the high thirties to the high seventies. The worst of the weather is an occasional spell of too much rain. Now and then there is a hailstorm. It is an indication of Cusco's moderate weather that the locals complain of being either too cold or too hot if the temperature gets out of a 55 to 70 degree range.

The stories and sketches that follow began as email messages to friends back home in the U.S. Many of those friends urged me to keep the stories coming and suggested working up a book.

This is the book. It is not a guidebook, not a socio-logical treatise. It is simply a collection of the observations and experiences of a Gringo who has been hanging out in Cusco for a long time. There is an effort herein to connect present experience with the clouded history of this marvelous place. Most of the characters that run through these tales are real. A few are imagined. In order to protect the guilty, some of the real characters have fictional names. Most of the events recorded here actually took place in whole or in part. Some are entirely fictional, but spring from a kernel of truth.

Cusco is a repository of mystery. How can we know the truth of a civilization that had no writing, that kept the story of their culture in the Homeric tradition of songs-as-history? It has been said that after three generations, oral history has no accuracy. That's enough to cast doubt upon our given history of the Incas. But among oral histories, that of the Incas is uniquely suspect. The *Quipocamayocs*, those worthies who created and sang the songs of a king's era, of his deeds, were forbidden to create their songs until after the king had died. Herein, obviously lies a perfect formula for revisionist history.

The first time I saw the mighty redoubt of Sacsahuaman I had a sense of vast antiquity. It was like Stonehenge, only more impressive in its magnitude, mystery and graceful construction. The perfectly fitted stones of Sacsahuaman are all of different sizes and shapes, and most of those in the lower traces of its zigzag walls are huge. One of those stones has been estimated to weigh up to 300 *tons*. Most of the other walls in Cusco are made of relatively small stones laid in a linear fashion. No matter what the archaeologists tell us, I cling to the belief that Andean America is the site of human history much, much older than they would have us believe. Maybe so, maybe not. But mystery piques curiosity just as curiosity piques exploration. So carry on, dear reader. Explore the people, the lore and the history of "The Navel of the World."

THE STONE WHEEL OF KACHIQHATA

The Kachiqhata Quarries
(Upper center)

In the short span of one century, we are told, the Incas created an empire that rivaled in extent and governance that of the Romans. They supposedly built 20,000 miles of roads over rugged, mountainous terrain. They built innumerable rope bridges spanning impossibly deep gorges. And they built stone walls of such magnitude and perfection that they defy our under-standing, even in this day of such marvelous invention and construction.

They did all this without iron tools, without beasts of burden, without writing.... and they did it without the wheel.

"I know where there's a stone wheel," the guide said. "An Inca wheel."

He might as well have been dangling gold before a Spanish conquistador.

"It's got to be Inca," he said. "I don't think there were any Spanish going all the way up there and carving wheels."

We were drinking together in Norton Rat's Tavern in Cusco, Peru. Norton's overlooks the main square, the *Plaza de Armas*. There is a balcony where you can eat, drink and watch the never-ending spectacle below. The bar is big and comfort-able and is usually host to a bunch of interesting people from all over the world.

The guide's name was Doug and he wasn't exactly your stereotypical image of an Andean guide. No austere old hawk-beaked coppery-skinned Indian was Doug. No, this was an authentic clean-cut, nice-as-they-come, all American white-boy. He was fresh-faced and eager and had great teeth. He looked like a Land's End ad.

At that time, Doug wasn't a very experienced guide. His first assignment was to begin the following Sunday. He had to meet a group of hot-to-hike gringo tourists at the airport at 8:00 A.M and take them over the Inca trail. Doug was 29, but he looked to be about 18. He had come into the bar alone and I was alone and we were about the only customers there, so we got together and started trading Inca theories and fantasies.

"The wheel's at the quarries of Kachiqhata," he said. "That's where they got the stones to build the temple at Ollan-taytambo. And it's not a mill wheel. Mill Wheels have grooves in them, and this thing doesn't have grooves." He talked about holes drilled here and there, but his image was difficult for me to visualize. It was beginning to sound a little like an alien craft... or maybe Ezekiel's wheel. But Doug radiates such honesty and goodness that I willingly suspended disbelief.

Ollantaytambo (oy yan tie tambo), the village itself, is notable for being one of, if not the only, remaining village in Peru where people still live in buildings of classic, pre-colonial Inca architecture. Most tourists are unaware of this. What they come to see is an architectural jewel perched on a mountain spur a few hundred feet above the village. This construction is one of the most impressive stoneworks in the Andes. It is a temple/ fortress of exquisite and unique design. The reason it and other similar architectural sites in Andean Peru are referred to as "temple/fortresses" is because they seem to have been both. They were temples but they were also defensive redoubts for the next attack from the neighboring tribe that came around to slaughter you and yours and take your life, your land, your food and your women. This temple at Ollantaytambo is obviously unfinished, but what is there is Andean stonework at its finest. Huge blocks of rose rhyolite were brought from the Kachiqhata quarries high on a mountain across the valley. They were sledded a couple of thousand feet down the mountain, somehow transported through the river, dragged several hundred yards across a field or two, then brought up a colossal 380 yard-long ramp to the construction site. The quarry at Kachiqhata was the only place around where they could find this stone and if the Incas wanted a certain kind of stone for their construction, they would go to great lengths and heights to get it. Rose rhyolite is pretty stone. It is a dense and fine-grained volcanic rock that is a light salmon to pale pinkish yellow in color.

I had seen the stoneworks at Ollantaytambo, but I had never been to the quarries, so the trip seemed worthwhile, even without the alleged wheel.

I tell Doug, "I'll pay your expenses if you'll take me up there, but I can't hike it on foot. We'll have to get horses."

I have a fair collection of excuses for not walking. My left knee was trashed years ago by an unfortunate automobile-person encounter where I was the person. It has been operated on twice and is severely cartilage-challenged. But that's only the half of it. My entire right leg has been weakened and un-coordinated by a weird, voodoo neuropathy that I am certain was the result of an old girl friend sticking pins in my effigy. The fact that I had just turned 63 was incidental as far as I was con-cerned, but it was good for an added excuse if I needed one.

When I was in Peru six months ago, I had hoped to ride up to the quarries. For one reason or another, it didn't happen, but I did get hornswoggled into a hike on the other side of the river that I thought would ruin me. I have an especially hard time with uneven terrain and much of that hike was a scramble from rock to root to branch. Horses seemed like a much better idea. I assumed there was a horse path to the quarries and, at the worst; we might have to walk a little way to the wheel.

"No problem." says Doug. "We'll get horses. I'll call Señor Ponce in Ollanta. But the only day I can do it is Satur-day."

I was ready whenever he wanted to go. I have been coming to Peru off and on for almost 25 years. I love a mystery, and the stoneworks of the Incas are a magnificent mystery. These people, or their predecessors, could move 100+ ton stones for miles and miles and then fit them together with such pre-cision that you can't get a scalpel between them. They had no animals to help with the transportation because llamas were the biggest and strongest of their animals and if you ask a llama to carry more than 100 pounds, he spits at you. They created these marvels without mortar, and they did it without metal tools.

Doug went off to call about the horses while I continued to take up space at the bar. I had come here, come for the forth time in two years to photograph the ruins and to broaden my un-derstanding of the Incas. I am putting together a web site of text & pictures that will hopefully lure the reader into a deeper ex-ploration of this fascinating culture. I have taken hundreds of photographs and have read most of the translated writings of the old Spanish chroniclers. The deeper I dig, the more I realize how much there is to learn.

But for all my serious intent, somehow, on this trip, I had fallen into frivolous ways. I was putting in a lot of man-hours at bars and discos. I was having a fine old time and mak-ing lots of new friends, but I was feeling a little guilty. I wasn't doing much to move my web site forward, unless I changed the point of the project and called it "Disco Babes of Cusco." If Doug could take me to see something that most people didn't know about and that injected another bit of mystery into the stew, I might redeem myself in my final days here.

Oh boy. I had no idea what I was getting into.

Doug came back and announced that Señor Ponce could provide horses at 40 sols each. That was about eleven dollars and seemed to be a pretty clear bargain when you consider that the critters had to carry us up a rocky, treacherous slope to an elevation that was some 2,000 feet above our starting place. But there is a fierce bargaining nature that besets gringos in Peru. By now we had collected a few kibitzers and one of them insisted that 40 sols was just a beginning price and we should hold out for 20.

Doug leaves and I continue to take up space at the bar. But now I am a changed man. My mind is on fire. Disco Babes flee from my thoughts. *A WHEEL!* What the hell was a wheel doing up in the Kachiqhata quarries? Sometime before the Spanish Conquest in the

1530s, work on the shrine at Ollantay-tambo, with its gigantic megaliths, suddenly and mysteriously stopped. There are surmises about the reason for this happening, but any of them could, or could not be, true. Again, it is that maddening lack of written history that clouds the past.

The path of the stones as they were transported from the quarries to the temple is clear. There are minivan-sized blocks abandoned on the ramp up to the temple site, across the fields below and even submerged in the river. And, as I was to find out, there are huge stones, cut and uncut all the way up the mountain to the quarries. There is no evidence that the Spanish ever took stones from the quarries. You don't see that rose rhyolite in any colonial buildings. When the Spanish needed building materials, they just tore down some Inca structure and mortared those stones together to make a grand colonial church or a grand colonial casa. It would seem that when work ended on the shrine at Ollantaytambo, work also ended in the quarries.

By pure chance, my dear crusty Swiss friend René was coming to Cusco the next day with his girlfriend Victoria. I hadn't seen René since we trucked around southern Spain three years ago in his personally-modified Iveco van. I was expecting to be with them while they were here, but I couldn't imagine them wanting to join me on the wheel expedition. Their time was too short and there was too much else to see. Before their arrival we were in daily contact by email, so I proposed an itinerary. We would go to Ollantaytambo on Friday morning, the day after they arrived. That would give them a day to acclimate. The trip would take an hour and a half by cab. That afternoon we could tour the ruins then the next day they could go on to Machu Picchu and Doug and I would go up to the quarries.

The night before their arrival, I planned to get to bed at a reasonable hour, but fate intervened. A group of girl friends asked me to go dancing. I agreed, but told them I'd have to quit early. It was too much fun. We went to Ukukus, one of the many discos in the center of town. This is the disco of the locals. It is where the staffs of the myriad bars of Cusco go after hours. It's a good place to go if you want authentic. Way too much fun. Early ended up being early in the morning.

Around noon, I was awakened by René, banging on my door and yelling "Hey! Vake up, old man!"

I am in scraggly shape. While they practice breathing at almost 12,000 feet above sea level, I struggle to penetrate my haze and get dressed. They are hungry, so we head for a restaurant.

We head up the street called *Hatun Rumioc*. This is the street of the famous twelve-cornered stone, the jewel of what's left of the walls of Inca Roca's temple. The walls are a classic example of Inca polygonal stonework. The stone is a yellowish/ greenish diorite. The fit is perfect.

The twelve-cornered stone and the wall itself are magnets for vendors of all sorts, and for about a hundred yards we are running the gauntlet. At the entrance we are offered toasted peanuts and habas, crispy toasted and salted morsels that are the shape of butterbeans. On various and unpredictable days you may also have the opportunity to buy chile rellenos, empanadas, juice, candy, ice cream cones and granola bars. The last sold by what I believe to be the only Korean man in town. He assures you that these bars are great for the Inca Trail.

Once past this mini food court there are art and craft shops left and right. The *galeria de arte* on the right has a sign that says "Free Entrance," and often the proprietor is standing in front, his arm extended, palm up, inviting you to take advantage of this free entrance. I never go in. I don't have any more room in my house for art. But somebody must be buying, because art is proliferating in Cusco. It can be found in an ever-growing number of galleries. It is also in the street.. There are now almost as many street vendors of art as there are of post-cards, and many of them are selling their own paintings, some-times for as little as a sol (28 cents). They approach you opening their folders so that you can see their work. I always refuse. There isn't even room in my house for small art.

Just past the "Free Entrance" gallery, you are assaulted by shoeshine boys, as well as the aforementioned peripatetic art and postcard vendors. There is an old blind man sitting on the pavement, leaning against the wall. He is dressed in traditional garb, the colorful manta and the peaked knit cap with ear flaps. He plays a *charango,* an Inca mandolin. He plays one song and he plays it not very well. There is a cup before him. Occasion-ally I will drop a coin into it. He seems not to notice and keeps plunking away at his instrument... the same tune... the same tune. Sometimes he is joined by another old man who plays a flute, also not very well. They play the same song.

Two women in traditional garb with llamas in tow ask me to take their photo for a sol. They ask this whether I have a camera or not. There is a little girl with a lamb that is some-times in her arms, sometimes on a leash. The lamb wears a hat with flowers attached. The little girl also wants me to take her picture...for a sol. Also whether I have a camera or not.

An old woman leans against the wall, hat in hand, outstretched, moaning pitiably. Victoria gives her a few coins.

Toward the midway point in this 100-yard odyssey there is often a cluster of tourists examining and having their pictures taken in front of the twelve cornered stone. It is a truly remark-able thing, with its graceful curves and angles and its perfectly beveled edges. René, who has been a builder, stops to examine it. He runs his hands over it, looks closely at the joints and shakes his head in amazement. It looks soft as butter. On the rare times when the crowd is minimal, I run my hands over this beautiful, quilted wall, always surprised that it is so much harder than it looks..

Just beyond, on the right, an elderly woman with teeth so big and perfect they must be falsies, is standing close to the right wall, selling necklaces and pendants. She wears medium heels and a black skirt with white polka dots. She looks like someone you would see in a church in the U.S. She has an outstretched arm with locally made necklaces hanging all along it and in her hand. After many days of passing this lady and buying nothing, I began to risk a smile. Surprisingly, she doesn't use this as an opening to press a sale. *She thanks me for the smile*. It is a rare and appreciated gesture.

Women selling carved gourds and ponchos stalk the street whining, *Amiigooo*. And when I refuse it's always, *maybe tomorrow.*

Sometimes blankets of red and black and yellow and green are laid on the street to display jewelry and weavings. It is amazing stuff, but it is stuff I don't need. I've already bought nearly one of everything in this town.

At the crest of hill there is more food. Someone is sell-ing little plastic containers of yogurt topped with peaches. A woman sits on a step selling hot tamales from a basket, lined and covered with a warm towel.

Past this we are back into the peril of vehicular traffic and the street has changed its name. Triunfo, it is now, and our restaurant, Los Tomines is only a few doors down on the left.

Los Tomines means "The Jugs," or "The Jars." It has nothing to do with tits or ptomaine. The place is open and pleasant and has a jug motif. The back wall is adorned with a large ceramic of an Indian woman with jugs all about her. One of these jugs has an unusually large mouth and is the food pass-through from the kitchen.

I go here frequently, so the waiters know me. If they see me coming, they open the door and give me the palm-up sweep-in gesture. Juan and Raul are polite, friendly and gracious and would do honor to the best restaurants of Manhattan and Los Angeles.

Raul sweeps us to my favorite table. It is in the corner beside a window. It is my custom to sit at this table, positioned with the window at my back so that I can read. We take our seats and Raul offers a menu and stands by, bowed slightly, hands clasped together in the time-honored fashion of waiters all over the world.

René and Victoria peruse their menus.

"I suggest the *menú*. A menu here is a *carta*. A *menú* is the daily special, an inexpensive meal that is usually served from noon to 3:00. Most of the restaurants have a *menú*, but Los Tomines has one of the best.

Raul describes the *menú* options, and after a bit of struggle with the Spanish, we order. Warm bread and a spicy green sauce are brought first, and next the beverage, which today is *chicha morada*, a juice made from blue corn that looks and tastes much like grape juice. Then we get an entré, an appetizer of *Chilé Relleno* with lettuce, tomato and onion.   Next is the traditional soup with quinoa, potatoes, onions, carrots, lima beans, hunks of Alpaca meat and other vegetables I cannot iden-tify.   And then the main course, the "*Segundo*." A plate covered with grilled chicken or trout along with a mountain of *papas fritas*... french fries... and a salad of tomato, onion and cucumber. There is so much food that it overlaps on the plate. The salad and the meat are partially obscured by the *papas fritas*. On request they will make a sauce to order and mine is *picanté*, made with garlic and peppers. I can never eat all this food, so I usually leave with a take-out bag containing another meal for later, or for someone in the street who looks hungry.   René, who is rail-thin, devours everything. Victoria leaves a little.

The cost of this feast is approximately $2.00 apiece.

After lunch, René and Victoria go off to look at the ruins around Cusco, and I go off to have another look at my bed.

That night we all go to Norton Rat's Tavern and catch up on old times. My local friends René and Yheni come in. René is Dutch and Yheni is Peruvian. I introduce them and immediately the two

Renés are deep in conversation in German. Aside from having the same name, they have in common that they take great delight in the sport of insulting me, and referring to me as "Old Man."

We stay up way too late and don't get started until near noon.

As soon as we leave the hostal, I start hailing cabs and bargaining for the fare to Ollantaytambo. The more tattered the taxi, the lower the price. We finally get a deal that amounts to a little over $15. It is a Toyota that has been imported from Korea. It still has Korean lettering on the side.

The drive to Ollantaytambo is breathtaking. We drive up to a higher elevation past Poroy with its sidewalk *chicherone* venders, then out onto the plain. The rolling hills are a patchwork of impossible greens. Fluffy clouds linger in a deep blue sky. After forty-five minutes we can see snow-capped mountains rising on the other side of the sacred valley. Then, shortly, we drop down into the valley and enter the town of Urubamba.

From here it is only fifteen or twenty minutes to Ollan-taytambo. The mountains become steeper as we drive parallel to the Vilcanota River, which at some inexact point will become the Urubamba River. Soon we can see ancient Inca terraces, *andenes*, on the opposite riverbank.

We got to Ollantaytambo in time for a visit to the major ruins. It was René's first day at this altitude, but he handled it easily. To get to the temple/fortress of Ollantaytambo, you must climb two hundred and forty four stone steps. At the top there is an unfinished complex that is, in many ways, unique in Peru.

The centerpiece is a wall of 6 gigantic megaliths standing side by side. Between each of the megaliths is a narrow column of stacked fillet stones. And the whole thing fits together perfectly without mortar. The precision of the fit and the size of the stones are hallmarks of Inca stonemasonry.

Lower photo by Kurt Bennett

Yet there is something quite different about this work. There are motifs here that are more typical of the much older structures at Tiawanaku on Lake Titicaca in Bolivia. Nowhere else in Peru is there such a strong architectural connection to Tiawanaku.. This is significant. The Incas claimed that they originated at Lake Titicaca. But they never claimed creation of the stoneworks at Tiawanaku. It is said that when Inca Pachacutec saw the stone walls of Tiawanaku he ordered his stonemasons to use them as a model.

That night we went to Señor Ponce's restaurant to check out horse availability. The place was of green walls with flores-cent lighting. There was a TV showing something about the life of Jesus. The TV was very loud and a rapt group of family and friends sat watching it from the other end of the room. I asked about horses and was quoted a price of 40 sols for each. Just as expected. I said I'd think about it. I was hoping for a price re-duction before we left the place, but it didn't happen. This was my first mistake.

We went to dinner at a restaurant that wasn't there six months ago. *Cafe del Sol* is a culinary oasis in Ollanta. Irini is the *jefe*. Irini exudes care. Her eyebrows peak in the middle. The decor is nice. Lying on tables covered with Inca fabrics are old photos, local pottery and books about the area.

After a fine dinner, Irini sat with us. We told her that we were trying to find horses to ride to Kachiqhata and had been offered mounts at 40 sols each. She said that sounded reason-able. She also offered some other advice.

"Check to make sure they're well shod. Check to make sure they're well fed. Make sure they are rested enough to make the trip. It's a hard one.

"And whatever you do, don't let them give you the gray mare with the foal. The foal comes along and always wants to nurse and it's just impossible, not to mention pathetic."

The next morning we went to Señor Ponce's place for breakfast and to ask again for horses. We were told that horses had to be reserved the day before. So much for gringo parsimo-ny.

There were several nags being readied for action on the square. I went out to look at them and saw Irini, sitting on the plaza with her baby. When I told her that we couldn't get horses, she suggested we talk to Washi, who was a few yards away working with the nags.

"Washi!?," says I. "Is his real name Washington?"

Yes, it was the very one. Two years ago my friend Kurt and I were here and had met Washington. He pronounced his name "Washing-tone." He was 15 then, a clear-eyed and smiling boy who spoke serviceable English. Now he was Washi, suddenly a man and very much the busy guide. He wore a T-shirt with "Washi" inked on it.

Washi told us he could get 3 horses by 1:30. I pressed him to make it sooner, and he promised to get the horses to us by 1:00. Then he took off with the nags, who were carrying some large tourists who didn't seem to know much about riding.

Doug showed up, as promised, at 10:00. We knocked around for a while, and passed a shop that was selling walking sticks. René suggested it might be a good idea to get a couple. I saw no need for them. We were riding to the quarries, and a walking stick would only be in the way on a horse. René bought two anyway and gave me one. We went for lunch, and while we were waiting for the establish-ment to go out and kill the chicken and fish for the trout, René used his amazing multi-tooled Swiss Army Knife to smooth his walking stick. When he finished with his, he went to work on mine. All the while, I watched with be-mused detachment. A waste of time, think I. It's just going to make riding the horses more difficult.

We were served a few minutes before our appointment with Washi. I know that you generally need to add some slack to any appointment with anyone in Peru, nevertheless I gulped down my trout and hustled to the square. It was indigestion for naught.

Washi didn't show up until 1:45 and then he told us that he could only get two horses.

"Fine," I said. "We can take turns on the horses. I'm sure I can walk *some* of the way as long as there's a path." I was thinking of last year's hike on the other side of the river and the scrambling and how hard it was for me.

Washi goes for the horses, and I go for a walk in the direction of the quarries. "I'll meet you somewhere before the bridge," I tell him.

I wanted to have another look at one of the so-called *piedras consadas*, the "weary stones." These were gigantic monoliths that according to legend were just too tired to make it to their destination. I was interested in one particular and peculiar weary stone. This huge megalith has two rows of cups cut into the surface. When I was here six months ago, I was told that someone had written a paper theorizing that these cups were part of a transportation scheme. The cups fit over round rocks so that the megaliths rolled as if on ball bearings. It sounded pretty strange, especially since the cups were on the top of the rock, and it would be a beast to turn the rock over, but I am determined to examine every theory, so it seemed worth another look.

So I am walking down this very dusty road that parallels the ramp. I come upon a huge weary stone replete with modern graffiti. A little further on, I come to the stone of many cups. I climb up on it and have a good look. There they are: two rows of cups, or one row of pairs of cups. Most of the depressions are separated by a few inches, but one pair is joined. It looks like a pair of aviator's goggles or a pair of butt cheeks.

I try it out. I lie down and discover, to my amazement, that the cheeks of my butt fit perfectly into the butt-cheek cups. Not only that, my heels fit perfectly into another pair of cups, and furthermore, my shoulder blades fit into still another pair. And beyond even that, the surface of this rock is putting pressure on my back at the very point where my neuropathy originates. AHA! I think. It must be an ancient Rolfing table.

I lie there, feeling very comfortable and dreamy. There are gentle clouds playing around in the sky. The day is fine and I am fine. An old man comes along and tells me in a Spanish-Quechua patois that the stone I'm lying on is a *piedra consada*.

I told him I was going to the quarries of Kachiqhata.

"*Lejos*," he said to me. "Far."

No problem, I think. We're going on horses.

After a while there are still no comrades, and no horses, but I am content to lie here and sense my surroundings. The stone is massive and firm beneath me and the sun is warm. I wonder at the effort it took for men to move this 20-something foot-long monster all the way over here from the quarries.

It seems like a good opportunity to ask the Inca spirits to have a shot at curing my voodoo neuropathy.

I intone to myself, "Oh Sun, oh *Inti*, who has nourished us for lo these many years, who has provided warmth and food, may your rays from above penetrate and heel me."

"Oh mighty stone, so powerful beneath me, may the strength of the earth, of *Pachamama*, penetrate from below and heal me."

I realize that this sounds clichéd and banal, but I am not accustomed to praying to pagan deities and so may be somewhat lacking in verbal finesse.

I keep this up for half an hour or so, trying to muzzle my left brain so that perhaps a minor miracle might transpire.

Still no comrades and no horses. It's almost two-thirty. I'm ready to postpone the trip. I'll ask Doug to draw a map for Washi so that we can go tomorrow. Washi and Doug have both insisted that the round trip hike on foot is only three hours. With horses it should be even less. But austral winter is coming in and the sun sets early. It's down by 5:30 or 6:00. If we leave in the next fifteen minutes, we're still cutting it close.

Then, suddenly, here they come.

"Hey, old man!" René is in the lead. He passes me with the news that my horse is coming and that Washi has managed to get a third horse. "But Washi's horse is a pain in the ass," says René. "He don't want to go on this trip and Washi ain't too good at changing his mind."

Next comes Washi. Washi is not exactly an experienced equestrian and he's having a terrible time what with the horse making furious attempts at a U turn about every twenty yards.

And finally comes Doug, leading my horse.   He has passed Washi, who is still struggling with his reluctant gelding.

Doug is walking.   He's leading a gray mare.   And trotting along beside her is a sorrel foal.

The foal keeps going for her teats.

This seems like a clear sign to me.   Didn't Irini warn me about the mare with the foal?

"Doug," I say.   "I think it's getting a little late to begin this trip."   Then I lay out my map idea.

Doug's answer is succinct and unequivocal.   "You'll never find it."

I acquiesce without hesitation.   Whatever it takes, I am determined to see this wheel.   And I want to see it on this trip.   The next time I get back down here, Doug may be somewhere else.   It seems like a last chance.

I ask Doug to lead the mare up beside the Rolfing stone so that I can mount.   The stone is so huge that its height is level with the mare's back.

I rode horses so much in my youth that my legs are bowed. I rode hunters and jumpers that were of goodly size.   This mare was hardly more than a pony.   I wonder at the sorry horses they breed here in the Andes.   What ever happened to the seed of those steeds that carried the conquistadors?   The mare is sad, but the tack is sadder.   The saddle is a sort of McClelland with a high pommel and cantle and a slot running through the middle.   The stirrups are of insufficient width and are fronted with leather hoods so that your foot can only go in so far. They are made for those pointy-toed boots that cowboys wear. I am wearing wide waffle-stompers and the stirrups must be pounded onto my shoe. Whenever I put weight on it, my right foot falls out of the stirrup and it is almost impossible for me to get it back in without help..

So now, with all but Doug mounted, the American-Swiss-Peruvian expedition to the Kachiqhata quarries, struggling with reluctant horses, proceeds apace. Down the road a bit, we cut a left to cross the fields. The corn has just been harvested and here and there are neat rectangles of ears both white and yellow laid out to dry in the sun. To our left, we see more *piedras cansadas*, huge and pink, lying there for oh so long with the grass growing up all around them. They are like disconnected railway cars scattered along a lost track.

Doug is walking ahead of the procession. He is not walking, he is striding. "Without a backpack, I feel light as a feather," he says. It looks it. He is charged with energy and fortitude. I remember the feeling and I envy him.

We come to the river. The stones from the quarries had to get past this obstacle somehow. It has been theorized, and is still written in guidebooks, that the river was diverted then re-diverted to get the stones across. Then along came Vincent Lee, the intrepid architect and explorer who tried to duplicate the transportation of stones from quarry to construction site. Lee discovered that because of the round river rocks, it was easier to pull the huge stones across the river bottom than on dry land.

We cross the rickety old bridge and begin to climb the other side. We pass a house or two, and at each of them Washi and the inhabitants exchange words in Quechua. I'm not sure what they're talking about, but I think it has something to do with somebody's sister or cousin. Whatever, it all seemed very familial.

Quechua was the language of the Incas. It is still spoken

today by millions of people in the Andes. The Incas imposed Quechua upon all of their conquered subjects. If you were a personage of any importance and you didn't use Quechua in your transactions, you were a candidate for severe punishment. Sons of the conquered, those of consequence, were sent to Cusco to learn the *lingua franca* of the Andes.

The foal turns out to be more help than hindrance. I urge her ahead by swinging the end of my reins near her rump. She moves ahead and the mare hustles to keep up. By the time we cross the bridge and begin the ascent on the other side, it is three in the afternoon.

"Yo, René," I shout.

"Ya?"

"Somebody has a theory that these stones were moved by cutting cups in them and hauling them with round stones in the cups. Like ball bearings. What do you think."

"Vouldn't vork. The stones vould fall out whenever there was a depression in the ground."

Ah the Swiss. His answer makes sense to me. Besides, I am still convinced it is an ancient Rolfing table.

We come to a turn in the path. Doug confers with Washi. The way Doug hiked this mountain before was to go straight ahead. Straight ahead is damn near straight up. Washi says the horses can't make it that way. We must go a distance over to the right and then somewhere over there, way out of sight, switchback to the left. Already the trek is beginning to look longer than anticipated.

So far the ascent is gentle. We have climbed high enough to get a fine view of the valley and the river and the mountains that rise on the other side of the river. Washi points to a little settlement half way up the mountain opposite. We can see a path that leads up to it.

This used to be his home, he tells us. His home looks to be at least 1500 feet above the river. He had to hike from there down to Ollantaytambo and back every day. Washi doesn't have the body of the typical Andean. Most of them are short-legged and barrel-chested from eons of accommodation to this vertical, oxygen-weak environment. Washi's body is long and lean and he doesn't have ostensibly gigantic lungs. But Washi can walk with the best of them.

We come to the first steep ascent. My old gray mare struggles up the hill, sagging and wallowing like an old Buick with bad shocks. She makes pathetic groaning sounds. The foal has a try at her udders. I can't take it any more. I dismount. Screw it. I'll walk up the hill. It doesn't really look that far and I seem to feel a hell of a lot better than this pathetic, worn-out horse.

"Save the horses for the trip back," I say. "Coming down is harder than going up. I'll need them more then."

The others dismount, and with fragile vigor we set out afoot.

Doug, ever the cheery one, tells me that we needn't worry about darkness because there's a full moon tonight. I know that's not true. The moon is waning and won't come up until some time after sunset. How long after sunset, I don't know. I don't remember how many days it's been since full moon and I'm too preoccupied with getting my legs to work to calculate moonrise anyhow.

Doug leads, apparently still feeling light as a feather. René is next, behind Doug, but still ahead of me.

"Hey, René," I shout.

"Ya."

"You know what's gonna happen? When we get to that wheel, Doug is going to look at it and say, 'Well, it *looked* like a wheel the first time I saw it. It looks kinda square now.'"

"Ya," says René, laughing. "That's it."

We all laugh and plod ahead.

After a while, I realize that my assessment of the distance is way off. It's a long, long way up there and I don't even know where "up there" is. I trail further and further behind.

Washi has taken all the horses by the reins and is trying to lead them. As we climb higher and higher, I look down and see him struggling with the beasts.

The going is so precipitous and rough and difficult of purchase that I can't imagine climbing it on a horse anyway. Much of the time I'm grabbing at whatever bushes are there for lift. I figure Washi will give up on us and take the horses home. We're all a little pissed at him anyway for bringing us tired horses, and nobody has much faith in the boy.

It's getting harder and harder for me. Dancing is the only exercise I've had in the last three weeks. Our elevation is around 10,000 feet above sea level and the air is thin. My lungs burn and I breathe with deep gulps. My heart is ka-thumping like the timpani in the opening of "2001, a Space Odyssey."

BOOM-boom, BOOM-boom, BOOM-boom, BOOM- boom!

It feels ready to break out of my chest.

All *right*, I say to myself. It's about time you had an extreme experience, Richard. Your life has been too even. Time you should push yourself. So I proceed, still feeling pretty good, if pretty tired. The legs are working okay.

We continue onward and upward toward, we hope, the stone wheel. Doug, the vigorous young bastard, is out of sight. René, who smokes one thing or another all the time and coughs like he has emphysema, is way ahead of me.

Now I'm having a bitch of a time. One foot in front of another. One foot in front of another. One foot in front of another.

I think about the people who have climbed Everest. They deal with even thinner air and they're freezing their asses off. This is nothing compared to that. I think about the soldiers who were on the Bataan death march. If you quit on that one, you got a bayonet through the gizzard. The only bayonets I face are the cactus spines.

The sun is getting low. It will disappear behind the mountain maybe 30 minutes before sunset. I can only think now of getting to the wheel before dark. René waits for me to catch up.

"Don't worry about darkness, René. There's a big moon tonight."

"Dere's NO moon tonight," he says.

"Yeah there is. It'll come up a little after sunset."

"Bull shit! Dere's no moon tonight."

"Okay René, let's get on with it. Where's Doug?"

"Vey up dere somewhere. Vat's vith dese stupid guides." He gets in my face now. "DIS IS NO THREE-HOUR TRIP. MAYBE IT"S A THREE-HOUR TRIP FOR A TWENTY YEAR OLD." I can't tell whether he's really pissed or just messing with me.

"He's twenty nine," I say.

"IT'S THE SAME GODDAM THING!" says René. He is pissed. René likes to kvetch and this is one grand opportunity for kvetching. Nevertheless, he's probably right about the difference between twenty and twenty-nine. There's not much.

After about five more steps, I feel a sharp pain in my right ankle. I look down and see that two cactus thorns have penetrated my hiking boot and lodged themselves in me. I jerk them out and yelp. The damn things have barbed ends.

We climb. Looking down we can see the Urubamba River and the fields beyond and the mountain rising beyond the fields. I pause for breath and thought. The breath consumes me at first, and then some thought comes.

There was a big battle fought down there, across the river. It was the only major battle the Spanish lost. Manco Inca, once a puppet ruler for the conquerors, is now in revolt and holed up at Ollantaytambo. The Spanish send out a small contingent of horsemen and foot soldiers and a bunch of Indian auxiliaries to deal with the problem. They know Manco is there, but they've never seen Ollantaytambo. They've never even sent a scout. Big mistake.

They have a terrible time getting there. The path along the Urubamba River changes from side to side and every crossing of the river involves a battle with the Indians. When they finally get to Ollantaytambo, they are faced with an im-possibly steep climb to the temple/fortress where Manco is ensconced. There are archers and stone-throwers and lancers all over the slopes. Not only that, the Indians have by now acquired horses and harquebusiers and know how to use them.

After enduring a hail of rocks, spears and arrows, the Spanish finally decide that this campaign is a bad idea. As they retreat, and the Indians, seeing a sign of weakness, mount a furious counterattack. And they have a secret weapon. Manco has arranged for a system to divert the river onto the fields to flood the enemy. The horses are mired, sometimes up to their bellies. But the Spanish somehow manage to get to the river and begin their retreat. The battle to get back to Cusco is harder than the initial incursion. The Indians had sprinkled thorny agave cactus over the paths to wound the horses. But the Spanish made it back. The conquistadors were rugged, fearless fighters, and luck (they would have said "God") was on their side.

I think about what a hard time the Spanish had and I think, "This climb is nothing. Those guys REALLY had a hard time."

Where we are going is somewhere between 2,000 and 2,500 feet above the river. From the other side, it didn't look so high.

Most of the time there is no path and the mountain is rocky. We see cut stones of varying shapes. Here a block, there a column, all over, many medium-sized stones, and everywhere, pebbles that are like ball bearings underfoot.

My right leg is getting tired of this drill. It doesn't want to work. I curse it. "Get up, you lazy piece of crap!"

One foot above another. One foot above another. One foot above another.

The heart is still beating out *2001* and I am pumping this thin air in and out of my lungs with frightening depth and speed.

Be glad this isn't the Bataan death march, I think. Along with everything else, they had dysentery. You've got it easy, pal.

René comes to kvetch some more. "Dis is crazy," he informs me. "It's getting late. Remember, DERE'S NO DAMN MOON TONIGHT! How're we going to get down dis fucking mountain in the dark?"

I'm trying to get my right leg to do my bidding. I'm too exhausted to argue. I raise a tired hand and shoot René the bird. "I don't know, René. If I think about getting down, I won't be able to keep going up."

"We're never gonna get to that wheel. I don't think there even IS a wheel. This is a nightmare."

"Then why don't you turn around now and go home so I don't have to listen to any more of your pissing and moaning?"

"I'm not gonna leave you, old man. You'd probably get killed up here without me to help you."

"Is that what you've been doing? Looking after me?"

"Ya! Ya! Dat's it. If it wasn't for me giving you shit, you'd probably quit."

Quitting was out of the question. I was determined to see the wheel, and it never occurred to me that getting there and back, even in the dark, would kill me.

We start climbing again. It requires a tremendous willpower to make my right leg work. I struggle to another level and pause, hands on knees, gasping and cursing.

After a few more exhausting minutes I call out to René.

He stops and turns around. "Ya?"

I pull the camera bag from around my neck. "Take this. In case I don't get to the wheel before dark."

For a moment, I can tell, he is formulating a wisecrack. But for once, René relents. He takes the camera and sets off ahead of me.

I shout after him. "Do you know how to work it? Be sure to turn it on first. And pop up the flash. It's the little button on the left."

René pays me no mind. He is trudging ahead.

We are moving in the general direction taken by Doug, whom we haven't seen for about fifteen minutes. Suddenly we hear his voice. We look left and right and see nothing. Then we look up.

He's standing atop a knoll that at this moment looks to be about a thousand feet above us. "I've found it! Up here!" He is silhouetted against the sky, standing there like a triumphant Thor on the mountaintop, the son-of-a-bitch.

"Up here."

Like getting up there was no problem.

There is no path to "up here." It is a steep ascent strewn with rocks of rose rhyolite. They look like huge hunks of salmon. Earlier, René has asked me why they didn't just build the damn temple where the rocks were, instead of bringing them all the way down one mountain, across a river and through a field and up a ramp to another mountain. I had surmised that it was because the temple site was located on a promontory overlooking the delta of the Patacancha and the Urubamba and was probably considered a sacred place. Struggling now up this barren rock-strewn slope, I couldn't imagine even those magnificent Inca engineers attempting to build that shrine here.

René is plowing up the hill ahead of me. "René," I yell to him.

He doesn't even turn around. "Ya?"

" I think Doug was pointing down when he said he had found the wheel. Why don't we just walk around the hill rather than over it?"

"Na. Won't work. We gotta go up."

I'm too tired to argue with him, so I follow. We are walking into the sun's waning light and everything is in silhouette. Finally, we come to the top and there is no sign of wheel, no sign of Doug. We call out to him and his voice leads us, not down, not over, but up. More Goddam up.

Exhaustion is edging me into an altered state of consciousness. The sun is below the mountain now and everything is getting pink.

The golden light of dusk heightens the color of the stones that lie everywhere. It seems surreal. I tell myself that I've got to come back here with a fresh horse and enough time to really see things. I'm far too out of it to give this extraordinary place the attention it deserves. I can only put one foot up and then another. It's a laborious process.

Finally we see Doug again, standing above us again, with that triumphant Thor stance again that makes me want to strangle him. He speaks. "Come on up here and see this wheel! Well, sort of a wheel. It's at least round on the edges." He laughs.

Okay, ha ha. But the distance looks manageable. Doug's not nearly as far or as high as he was for his first Thor appearance. I can't see a wheel from where I am, but I think he is pointing to it and it looks like he's pointing to something right there beside him.

That rock wheel was not right there beside Doug. It was more UP. More mothableeping UP!

I am scrambling up the scree in spurts. The light is waning. I'm going to get to this wheel if it kills me, and I am going to photograph it. "René!"

"Yah?"

"Give me the camera."

He waits until I catch up. "Think you're gonna make it, old man?"

"Up yours. Give me that goddam camera."

He gives it to me and we continue. I figure René must be tired. It's been a while since I've heard any gratuitous grousing from him.

Then all of a sudden we are there.

And it *is* a wheel. It is not lying flat as I had expected. It is standing just a few degrees off the vertical. I activate the camera and flash. René immediately mounts the wheel and perches on the edge, wielding his walking stick like he's the king of the mountain. Doug stands beside the wheel.

I take a couple of pictures, then Doug, who's had enough of sharing the discovery, yells at René. "Get off there." After that, I have Doug take a picture of me at the wheel. I look as exhausted as I feel.

The wheel is 63 inches in diameter. The edge is beveled. There are holes drilled on-center, one from each side, that do not meet. The front hole is the larger of the two.

Part of the back of the wheel has split off and there is a hairline crack completely around the circumference just a couple of inches in from the front surface. Sooner or later the thing would have split again. This stone was layered and it was hardly the one to use for this purpose. I can't imagine the same people who built the temple having made such an egregious mistake. It adds to my belief that some of the art was lost by the time the Spanish arrived.

It looks sort of like a millstone, but I can't figure out why the holes are drilled from either face but do not meet. I imagine the thing careened down the hill from where it was shaped, careened down and lost major parts of itself. I wonder, did it land so perfectly like a standing picture frame? Or did someone with a fine eye take the time to set it up so nicely for future generations to admire?

But there is no more time for conjecture or photography. The light is getting frighteningly dim. We begin our return.

We have gone only a few yards when we hear a whistle. We look up to see the totally unexpected. On a ridge above us is Washingtone. And he has the horses. They actually made it up there. Washingtone is like his namesake, the general himself, ready to lead us across the Delaware. We shout to him and he motions that he will bring the horses around. He indicates "around" with his hands and it looks like a long way around. He is pointing to a path that is way below us.

Doug, René and I begin a pell-mell scramble down the hill. As usual, I hold up the rear. Going down is worse than climbing up. At least it seems that way now. I am falling a lot. The slope is rife with pesky little pebbles that deny me purchase. I announce now that I have a flashlight. I pull out a finger-size maglite that runs on a single AAA cell. I have no spare batteries. Other than a couple of Bic lighters, this is our only light. No one considered it necessary to bring a flashlight. After all, it was only supposed to be a 3-hour trip. The only reason I have one is because the little thing was already in my pocket. I am determined to continue without it as long as possible. We have a long way to go in the dark.

The light goes from pink to colorless, and as it diminishes, so does my balance. I am staggering as though besotted and don't have much faith in my ability to negotiate this treacherous descent without help. It's another trick played on me by this vile voodoo neuropathy. Doug is ahead of me. I call out to him. I have this idea. I ask him to hold one end of my walking stick while I hold the other. It works. My balance, borrowed from Doug, returns.

When we finally meet up with Washing-tone and the horses, there is scant light left. But now there are two new people with us: a boy who couldn't possibly be over ten and another about Washi's age. It was their home we passed on our way up. They have realized that we are in trouble and have come to help. Washi has René take the reins of two horses while he and his friend strategize. They are speaking in Quechua and the clicking sound of that strange language in this strange, dark place comforts me. I don't understand the words, but it is obvious that they are trying to decide the safest way out of here. Washi has been here many times, but he's never had to get home in the dark.

They decide that we should not return the way we came, but should take the long way. The long way path is a long way down from where we are and there's no possibility of riding horses down that slope. They must be led. Suddenly the boys move. They tell René to follow them with the horses. In the few remaining minutes of light they must get the horses to the path.

Doug and I set out to follow. Once again I am the holdup. We are using the stick trick to keep me in some semblance of balance. Finally it is so dark that I have to use the little flashlight. I turn it on and stick it in my mouth. It illuminates only a few feet ahead of me, just enough for the next step or two. This is beginning to look like it could be a genuine life-threatening experience. Whatever I thought about the difficulty of that hike last year, it was nothing. *This* is something. Too much something.

I come to a clearing, a little level place on this unforgiving slope of ball bearings. I stagger around a bit and sit down. I have a poncho in my backpack. I know the moon is going to come up *sometime* tonight, and I'd a hell of a lot rather wait for moonlight than to continue with this madness. I can see me stumbling to my death; or at least to a damaged body part. I tell Doug I'll give him the flashlight and I'll stay here till moonrise. But he'll have none of that. We have to keep going.

Doug tries to encourage me. Or maybe he's encouraging himself. "You know, whenever something like this happens, the day ends up with everybody sitting around a fire talking about what a hell of an experience it was." That seems to me the most likely end to this saga. I never once think there will be dire consequences to this night ride. Why I think this, I can't tell you, for in truth, there is ample opportunity for tragedy. There are no precipitous cliffs where you could fall hundreds of feet to your death, but there are so many *rocks*. Rocks to trip you, rocks to slide on, and steep slopes strewn with more rocks to break your head or your bones.

Now there's another problem. It's totally dark and Doug is unsure of the direction we should take to connect with the others. We continue in the general direction of down and keep shouting to them. We can hear René calling to us, but we can't tell where his voice is coming from. We keep yelling and I wave the flashlight.

"Where are you," yells Doug. "We can't see jack."

René flashes his Bic to give us a fix on his direction. It is impossible to tell how far down he is but it looks close. I see lights somewhere behind them and assume that they are coming from one of the houses we passed on the way up. That would mean we are pretty far down the mountain. No such luck. Those lights are coming from way across the river. We still have a long trek ahead.

An hour after René and the others left with the horses, Doug and I finally get to them.

I have a few yards to go. It's still down and still rocky and precipitous. I place my stick on what appears to be solid ground and lean on it.

It is not solid ground. The stick gives way and I go into a somersault down the hill. I'm in mid air and my head hits a rock. Strangely enough, it doesn't seem to hurt much. I wonder if it's worse than it feels. I land on my back and go into a downhill slide. It all seems very slow and dream-like. Suddenly Washi is there trying to brake my fall. He catches me in his arms and the two of us continue sliding down the hill. When we finally stop, Washi says something that sounds like "concussion". He gets a firm grip on my arm and leads me around like he's a cop hanging onto his prisoner. I wonder what a concussion feels like and if I might possibly have one. After a bit of this being dragged around by Washi, I tell him I think I can make it better if he'll just loosen his grip on my upper arm.

When we get to the horses, René says, "This is the part where we throw you over the saddle."

"Ha, ha, René. Very funny." Actually, if René stopped insulting me I would figure he didn't like me any more.

Our entourage now includes three gringos, three Peruvians, three horses and one foal. The Peruvians form a plan. The gray mare, the one with the foal, will go first, and Washi's friend will lead her with the help of my flashlight. They reason that the other horses stand a better chance if they have a light-colored horse to follow. Only René and I ride. Doug, who isn't too comfortable with horses, leads my horse.

The horses, sensing that down means going home, are no longer so recalcitrant. It's a good thing because we still have a lot more down to cover before we get to the path that will take us home. Now is when I *really* hate these stirrups. As my horse picks his way through the rocks and down one steep incline after another, I lean back, put the weight on my feet and repeatedly, the right foot falls out of the stirrup. It still beats hell out of walking.

Doug is ahead of me, trying to lead my horse, but I think the truth is that the beast doesn't need any leading. He's following the gray mare. Doug is having a terrible time. He slips and slides every few steps. He is wearing a dark jacket and it is now so dark that there are times when I cannot see him. I think he is taking a left turn only to realize that he has actually turned right. Doug, in his slipping and sliding, is no longer quite his Thor-like self, but he carries on and complains not.

I had forgotten how well a horse can traverse difficult terrain. My gelding is picking his way down through the rocks very nicely. He is doing a lot better than Doug.

René yells to me, "Dese horses are doing pretty well."

"That's because they have four legs," I say. I am, after all, the horse expert in this group.

"Dat's three more legs dan you have."

We laugh. "Good one, Ren."

"Ya," he says. "I tell you this. I'm glad it's dark, because if I could see I'd be scared to death."

I had thought about that on the way up. The path is just a narrow ribbon etched into the steep slope.

When I was here six months ago, I had wanted to see the southern sky the way the old Incas saw it. We who live anywhere near a city have lost our skies to electric lights. But in this darkness and thin air the stars seem very close and very clear. It is so clear up here that the Incas envisioned some of their mythological animals in the Milky Way. They didn't see them in the stars, but in the dark clouds of interstellar gas that punch holes in the sparkling swath of our galaxy. Six months ago the viewing was poor. Now the viewing is patchy, but where there are no clouds, the sky is magnificent. The Southern Cross is low on the horizon, and near it the Milky Way billows up from behind the mountain, rising to thirty degrees where it disappears behind the clouds. It sparkles over us with an intensity and depth that stuns the eye.

We come to a clear path and the local boys leave us. I thank them and give the older one 20 sols. That's about $5.81 U.S., and a bona fide bargain for getting saved from what could have been truly dire straits.

Finally we see signs of civilization below us. There is a string of lights that seem to float in space. It looks like the bridge to me. Thank God. Finally.

But it's not the bridge. It is another fifteen minutes before we realize that what we are seeing is streetlights on the short road from the railway station to the town. The station was hidden from us. Now we can see it just a short distance away... but across the river. We are so close, but still so far. The bridge is nowhere near.

Now we are down close to the river. This is where I hiked last year. Silhouettes of dimly remembered features loom up into the night sky. Starlight is our only illumination. Exhaustion clouds my awareness and casts a dream-like state over everything..

It is the end of the rainy season, the end of their summer, and the river is swollen. I think of the next chapter in the efforts of the Spanish to quell Manco Inca's rebellion. They didn't quit after that first disastrous attempt at Ollantaytambo. They were a persistent lot, the conquistadors, and they weren't going to let their only big defeat in Peru go unanswered. They were determined to put an end to Manco.

They waited for reinforcements and then they came back. But Manco knew they were coming, and he had fled deeper into the jungle. The Spanish pursued, but Manco eluded them. The same could not be said for his wife, who was captured and brought back to Ollantaytambo.

The Spanish were frustrated and furious. And just to show it, they stripped Manco's wife, whipped her, and shot her naked body full of arrows. Then they stuffed her tattered corpse into a basket, which they set out on the river, knowing that it would come to Manco. And Manco would know that they meant business.

Manco was eventually killed, not in battle, but by duplicitous Spanish assassins. That pretty much ended the Inca rebellion and consolidated Spanish rule in Peru.

When René and I were up at the temple site yesterday, he said something I won't forget. I told him that these huge stones for the sun temple came from across the river and up the mountain opposite. I pointed to the Kachiqhata quarries.

He laughs, "HA! HA! HA!" That's the way René laughs. It's like a bad reading of a script. "Dese guys really had it coming. HA! HA! HA! Think of what they could have done with all that energy."

Maybe so. But I don't think it would have changed the course of history. The Spanish had the horse and fine steel swords and were the best soldiers in sixteenth century Europe. Disease and civil war had already weakened the Incas. They were no match for the conquistadors.

It makes me sad to think of a civilization of such incredible achievements in agriculture and construction and governance being so thoroughly obliterated. But that was the way it was. And in some ways, that is the way it still is.

We finally got back to town at nine o'clock. We were all exhausted, except, perhaps, for Washi. He's used to this. All the horses but mine were stabled on the way to the central plaza. While they were being put away, I rode on alone.

A huge truck is coming up behind me on this narrow street and there is not room for it and my horse. I continue and the truck is forced to move at horse speed. With the bright headlights behind me, I sit tall in the saddle for my entrance. There is a crowd waiting. They are gathered around the owner of my horse who has been there for hours waiting for his animal. I dismount and a group of boys crowd around me to gawk and ask about my bloody head.

Washi and the others arrive. It is time to pay up. I am expecting an appeal for more than the figure agreed upon, but he keeps to his price... twenty sols. Forty sols would have gotten us up there and back long before dark. Lesson learned.

We pick up René's girlfriend, Victoria, who is pretty calm considering we are 3 hours late. We go back to Café del Sol. Washi is already there and Irini has given him a large ration of grief for taking us up there so late on tired horses, especially when one of them is the gray mare with the foal.

We all have dinner. We take pictures. Washi says to me, "*Tu es fuerte.* You are strong. Your leg hurt but you wouldn't quit." It makes me feel good.

* * * *

We all lived. And that is the end of it.

Except for a footnote or two:

You may be wondering about the effectiveness of my prayers to the Inca gods while I lay upon the big Rolfing stone.

Did it work? I can't be sure. I climbed a mountain that I thought was surely an impossibility for me. Sufficient evidence perhaps, but who knows? Perhaps prayer to Inca gods had nothing to do with it. Inti and Pachamama, as powerful as they were in their time, may well have expired with the rest of the Inca civilization.

When I got back home I went straightaway to the best source I have on Ollantaytambo; Jean-Pierre Protzen's, Inca Architecture and Construction at Ollantaytambo. I am breathless to see if he has knowledge of the wheel. It would be so fine to tell him something new.

But, alas, he does know about it. He mentions it briefly in his chapter on the Kachiqhata quarries:

"A lone millstone, not quite completed... testifies to colonial presence in the quarries."

That's all. It was no big deal.

EL LORO

My bedroom has a window that overlooks a pretty piece of Cusco. I've set up a table in front of this window for my computer. I can look away from the computer screen to the terra-cotta roofs and the towers of several churches and the mountains in the distance. The window faces south, so I can watch the changing patterns of light on the mountains as the sun makes its crossing.

Just outside the window two things are going on. Don't look for any clever literary juxtaposition here. These things just *happened* to be happening at the same time, so I'm going to write about them at the same time.

In what was formerly a garden, there is construction afoot for additions to this little apartment complex. For many days now, laborers have hauled materials to the site, hauled them on their backs and shoulders without machinery or beasts of burden. Sometimes they have to haul them from the corner down the block, which is about a hundred yards away. I've done some construction work in my time and I feel for these men who work all day, carrying heavy loads on their backs.

The other thing that's going on is my relationship with this parrot. We are bonding, this bird and I. He perches in the upper branches of a wispy little tree just outside my window. This tree is hardly more than a bundle of twigs because this parrot, this *loro*, has stripped it of most of its leaves. Whether the branches are stripped for food or for better purchase, the effect is the same.

I don't know his proper name, so I will use the Spanish generic, *Loro*, for my fine-feathered friend. Loro is stunningly beautiful. He is as green as the hills and sports little splashes of brilliant red and blue on his wings. He has a white mask and the crown of his head is an iridescent blue-green. His beak is black and it has the curve of a scimitar. If I were a female parrot, I would go for this guy.

Loro is great to look at, but he's not much of a talker. A monosyllabic squawk is all I've heard from him.

So, in the name of experiment, I have taken it upon my-self to teach him proper English. I'm not going to teach him "hello," or "Poly want a cracker." I am going to teach him to say "Attention." That's all.

I got the idea from Aldous Huxley's novel, "Island." On this eponymous island, there are many parrots and for a very clever reason the human inhabitants came up with a wonderful idea. They decided to teach the all the parrots one word, one word only, and that word, of course, is "attention." This is so that when you are out and about on the island you are apt to be startled by an unseen parrot shrieking that admonition. Shocked into attention, so to speak. The message is clear. Keep your eyes and ears open so you don't miss an astonishing bird-song, or a splendid sunset. And also so that you don't fall over a log or get run over by a truck.

I know horses and cats and dogs, but I am a bird-virgin. I have never attempted to train a parrot to speak and I'm begin-nine to wonder if I have the talent. It is slow going. My first act of the day is to open the window and confront Loro. He is usually there, clinging to the pathetic, denuded branches of his tree. Loro on his twig and I at my window are at just about normal conversation distance.

"Attention!" I say.

"Grark," is his response.

"Attention!"

He cocks his head to the side. "Aaark." He has one claw wrapped around two thin branches he has twisted together to make a stronger perch. He scratches his head with the other claw in a motion fast as hummingbird wings.

"Attention!"

"Garrk."

Like that. It's discouraging.

One day Loro wasn't there when I opened the window. So I set aside the language lessons and put my attention to the construction of the new apartment wing.

Today the task is to raise a big pole and slide it into the hole that's been dug for it. This will be one of the main supports of the building, which will hang from such poles. In the historic center of Cusco, all construction is supposed to be in the old style, which means that the materials shall be adobe, bamboo, plaster, terra-cotta tiles, mud, eucalyptus and a very heavy, strong wood called *chonta*. This pole to be erected is made of *chonta*.

There are about ten workers assigned to this pole erection. It seems like there's no leader and no plan. It looks like a public works project. There is a lot of perplexed standing around and head scratching. Then, after extensive cogitation and consultation, posed like marines raising the flag at Iwo Jima, they get one end of this pole up a few feet and scotch it with an X-shaped truss. They take a break, then, ever so slowly; they raise the pole higher and higher, awkwardly shoving the truss forward. Finally they get it up high enough to attach a rope and pulley. It's not a block and tackle, a complex pulley system that magnifies force and has existed for centuries. No, they are just using a simple rope and pulley. It was like Newton had never existed. I watched six men hang onto the rope with their eight or nine hundred pounds of force with no results. After a while I couldn't stand it anymore. I went to the *dueño* of the apartments and suggested using a block and tackle to raise that pole and all the others that awaited erection so that the project might get completed before the next millennium. The *dueño* doesn't speak English and I don't know the words in Spanish for "block and tackle," so I draw it for him. But either he didn't get it or he couldn't find a block and tackle in town, or he just didn't want to bother, because a block and tackle never showed up. It's probably a make-work thing.

If I may say so without offending my hosts, I think they need better management. Obviously, before the conquest, they had it. How else could they have built all those 20,000 miles of roads, fabulous agricultural terraces and unequalled stoneworks? Management is where the Incas excelled. Like the Romans.

Now mind you, most of the people who lived here before the conquest were not Incas. The Incas were a small ruling clan that told their subjects *exactly* what to do and when and where to do it. Think Saddam Hussein's Baath party.

When the Spanish came along they either killed or emasculated the rulers...the Incas...the *managers*. The Spanish replaced the Inca concept of management with their own. Nurtured on the techniques of the inquisition, their idea of management was the whip. It was a poor replacement. The results linger to this day.

Nevertheless, the next day the pole was in position and it looked like a holiday because no one was working. Loro, however, was back on the scene, so we could resume our language lessons. But it was dismal. It seemed Loro didn't even care. When I say "attention," in my very best parrot voice, Loro looks the other way. Whether this is an expression of either disdain or disinterest, it is not a good sign.

It went on like that for a few more days and I began to wonder if it is possible for a parrot to say "attention." I'm thinking it's something akin to the difficulty Asians have with the letter "l." If a parrot doesn't have the vocal equipment to say the word, "attention," then Aldous Huxley has cruelly deceived me. I have always been a Huxley fan, especially a fan of his novel "Island," which was a retort to his to his earlier novel, the mechanistic utopia, "Brave New World," required reading in many a lit course.

Some time after writing "Brave New World," Huxley had some experiences that turned his head around about mechanistic utopias. His epiphany occurred sometime in the sixties, when he and Gordon Wasson, Tim Leary and that crowd got into psychedelic mushrooms down in Mexico. I think they were ingesting the *Amanita Muscaria*, the big red one with white dots, the "Alice in Wonderland" mushroom.

The *Amanita Muscaria* is a dangerous fungus. It can make you very sick, maybe even kill you. In some mushroom cults, the ordinary people didn't eat the mushrooms. The priest ate the mushrooms and the people drank his piss.

Anyway, Huxley didn't die from eating the mushrooms and I find it hard to believe that such a cultured man of letters from such a fine old English family would be drinking any priest's piss. Whatever, the mushrooms changed his life. He saw the world differently and expressed it in his novelistic concept of a humanist utopia, "Island."

As I am writing this, my attention is diverted by an extraordinary sunset. A low-lying cloud is turning everything red. And here comes Loro, beak and legging his way up his tree. Roosters are crowing in the distance and Loro is squawking back at them in a fair imitation of rooster-talk. I wonder, can it be that much harder to speak English?

I open the window and shout, "**Attention!**"

He looks at me and replies, "Graak awkk."

I take this as a small measure of success. The creature has leapt into polysyllabism.

As it turns out, my enthusiasm was premature. I got the truth from my old friend Patrick after having sent him a photo of Loro. Patrick has not only cohabited with various birds, he has studied them in all their beauty and variety and has painted many a splendid watercolor of real and imagined creatures of the air.

After a glance at the photo, Patrick told me this: Loro was a macaw, and though macaws are of the same family and may look sort of like a parrot to the half-blind or simply *inattentive*, the fact of the matter is, macaws don't talk like parrots.

Getting up in the morning is number two on my hate-list of mandatory daily chores. Number one is going to bed.   But the morning following the macaw revelation was especially shitty. My illusions had been shattered. I had been branded *inattentive*.

I could not bring myself to look out the window. I went downstairs to the kitchen and made breakfast. It was the first time I had cooked *anything* in this apartment. And as I went through the automatic breakfast preparations, my mind was ever on that window. In my mind's eye, I could see that non-parrot, that *macaw* and those fifteen or so guys struggling with another pole erection. An uncontrollable anxiety swelled in me. I left my cross-eyed fried eggs untouched. I raced up to the second floor, to the window. It was just as I had imagined it would be. The non-parrot was there as were the workers, struggling with another pole. I threw up the window, filled my lungs and screamed at us all:

ATTENTION!

Some months later I witnessed an event that made me want to retract some of what I had written. It was in the Plaza de Armas and it was well into the night. A strip down the center of the street was cordoned off and the cobbles had been removed. A line of men were digging a trench three or four feet wide. Relentlessly, they wielded pickaxe and shovel under the direction of a foreman. The next morning the street was back to normal. The cobbles had been replaced so that you could hardly tell they had ever been removed. And the next night a new strip, just beyond the first, was getting the same treatment. They were laying a conduit, working through the night so as not to disturb the traffic. It was an operation as slick and well managed as any I have ever seen.

Hope springs...

THE BALCONY

*A window on the center
of the Navel of the world*

At this moment I think my favorite place on earth is the *Plaza de Armas* in the center of Cusco. I like to sit on the balcony of Duffy's Place to take it all in from a second floor perspective. The view is world class. From here I can watch the sunsets. I can see the fountain backlit and sparkling in the afternoon sunshine. And at anytime of day I can watch the unceasing flow of humanity.

I've been coming to Duffy's Place for longer than any other watering hole in Cusco, and I feel a proprietary interest in the place. I also consider Duffy, who is American, to be a good friend. I want the rest of the world to know the pleasures of this vista, so I am always on Duffy's ass about improving the place so that he can capture the balcony clientele that his establishment deserves.

My first offer was to refurbish and promote the balcony for some percentage of the balcony business. Old Duff wasn't about to go for that.

"I don't have any way of separating the balcony business from the rest of the business."

Okay, I can buy that. But still, night after night I stand or sit on this rare and wonderful window to the center of activity in the western hemisphere's oldest city, this crossroads of the world, this magnet for the deeply curious and adventurous. And I feel a passion, such a passion for this balcony that I am almost ready to fix the place up as a gift.

Other balconies on the Plaza usually seem to do better business than Duffy's. Duff complains about it. One day I suggested hanging flowers from the ceiling of the balcony. It would add color, attract the eye, and perhaps attract customers as well. Duff liked that idea and started considering how many pots he had and what flowers he would plant in them. Weeks passed and no flowers were hung. One day I asked him where the flowers were. He pressed his lips into a line and said nothing.

Another week or so passed. Then one night Duff gave me a stack of CD's he wanted me to copy on my computer. He also gave me the blanks.

"What's in it for me?" I say.

"Well… you told me you would do it for me. What do you want?"

"I want you to hang those flowers on the balcony!!"

There is a long pause. Duff was busily tweaking the vanes on one of his precious, titanium darts. He was making that very, very, thin horizontal line with his mouth.

"Okay, Duff, what about it? Agree to that?"

Another pause as Duff aligns the vanes. Then, mum-ling, "Weeell, if you want a few drinks, that's okay, but there's no way you're going to bribe your way into management of this place."

"Bribe your way into management of this place!"

I love it. A classic retort. I complemented him on the literary qualities of the line and then blew loudly into his ear, "YOU ARE THE WORST CASE OF *'LET ME DO IT MY-SELF MOTHER'* THAT I HAVE EVER KNOWN!!!!"

Sheesh! What a jerk. I retreat to the balcony. The ballet of the *Plaza de Armas* continues. I am leaning on the balustrade, which is desperately in need of refinishing. Hunks of scabby paint cling to the bare wood. I am irked. This is one of the finest pieces of real estate in the world and it is not getting the attention it deserves.

From here, parts of five churches are visible. Beyond and above the plaza, the lights on the hill of Santana, glisten like blue and white stars.

The *Plaza de Armas* is vibrant.

This plaza was always vibrant, even before the Spanish changed its name to *Plaza De Armas*.

The Incas called it *Huacaypata*, the Place of Tears. It was the plaza where the Inca forces collected to prepare for war. It was larger then. Now the cathedral and the arched walkways intrude upon the great space that was once there.

Huacaypata. Or, depending the writer's notion of how to render an unwritten language: *Huakaypata, Wakaypata, Aukaypata*, and no doubt many others. There was a great monolith standing somewhere in its midst. The surface of the plaza was covered with two feet of sand that was brought by human carriers from the Pacific coast beach a few hundred miles and scads of mountains away. Beneath the sand were channels to carry away the effluvia: The vomit and the urine of those celebrating the advent of war by getting wretchedly drunk on *chicha*, their maize-based brew, that to this day inebriates legions of campesinos daily.

Now, here in the present, comes the nightly train of street cleaners crossing the park. They are all in orange ... orange overalls, orange masks over their faces and orange caps. Printed on the backs of their overalls is their identity. SELIP: *Servicio Limpieza Publico*. They are all pushing orange fifty-gallon trash containers that are rigged like wheelbarrows. A while back in the recent past, the administration of this city decided that tourists might like it better if the city were clean. And clean it is now. The SELIP minions are ever on the job. They are vigilant. They are proud of their work. Once I saw a parade of all the people who worked for the city of Cusco. First came the mayor, standing proudly in the back of a pickup truck, a raised hand waving, a yellow sash across his business suit. Then came the office workers in their suits, attempting a goose-step. It went on and on and finally ended with the garbage trucks, followed by the minions of SELIP. They were a sporty lot, all wearing bandanas around their necks, and they stepped smartly, stepped with a pride unmatched in that parade.

Since my first visit in 1975 this town has changed. Not only is it cleaner, it is way better lit. It is harder for thieves to operate at night. Recently, there has been a proliferation of upscale jewelry stores replacing cheap restaurants and handicraft shops.

What other city in the world can compare to this? It is ancient and modern all at the same time. The girls in their bells walk the same streets with women in indigenous Inca Garb, leading their Lamas and offering the opportunity to photograph them for one sol.

Campesinos crowd the streets, hawking their native crafts while young Cuscueñans crowd the internet *cabinas* to interact with the world at large.

The primitive and the modern ... side by side, just as the old Inca walls and the colonial Spanish architecture exist today in horizontal layers.

Oh, how I love this place. I love it for its architecture, for its flow of humanity from all over the world, for its weather, for its architectural and geographical beauty, and especially for its incipience. Cusco is relatively undiscovered, and I can see from year to year the ongoing discovery. Cusco is safe and inexpensive and mysterious and historical and impressive.

I love the plaza especially when it is wet. Then, there is a lambent beauty here, with the squiggly reflections of the streetlights on the pavement, the silhouettes of the people and their shadows, the patterns of light on the cobblestone streets. The street was wet tonight, but there was, for the moment at least, no rain. A group of pretty young girls cross the park, laughing all the way. They are arm in arm. A delicious bouquet of curves they are. They walk tall and straight. They are graceful. They move together with an easy, synchronized pace. I sigh with joy. Now comes a counterpoint...a trio of gringas amble down the street. They have frizzy, bleached-blond hair. They are not walking arm in arm. They have their arms crossed tightly beneath their breasts. They walk with an assortment of wobbles. Their stride is neither synchronized nor graceful.

After a bit of rumination on the varieties of human bipedal locomotion, I looked left and right and saw no one. The balcony was mine. It was all mine. This most excellent vista. This window on a most remarkable piece of the world.

Why on earth would I want to get anybody else up here? If the world knew about it, there wouldn't be room for me and I would have to find another vista. And surely, it would be a lesser one.

I go back into the bar. Duffy is still fine-tuning his titanium darts, lavishing selfless love upon them. I seat myself beside him and order another drink. Then, after an appropriate pause I say, "Now really, Duff, in all seriousness, when are you going to do something about that balcony?"

He barely glances at me but the lips draw a little tighter and straighter. He says nothing. Well, I figured, if that was meant to be reverse psychology, it didn't work.

A few weeks after I had returned to the states, I got an email message from Duffy. He wanted me to pick up this special, really deadly slingshot for him. He aimed to murder a few pigeons that were crapping on his stairs.

His message ended with a casual aside.

"The balcony is almost finished."

FLACO

Flaco is a drug dealer.   I knew this about him before I knew his name, because the first thing that came out of his mouth when we met was an offer.

It was four years ago in Aguas Calientes, the little town where most overnight visitors to Machu Picchu find food and lodging.   I visited this town for the first time many years before. It was 1975. Aquas Calientes was primitive.   My friends and I got shelter and beds for ninety-seven cents each. There was no toilet in our place. I think the only toilet in town was a latrine.   It was a long one covered with a concrete slab punctured in the appropriate places with holes and foot purchases.   It was the communal toilet, a ten-holer at least and it was ghastly beyond description. Apparently nobody in Aguas Calientes could aim.

Flaco means "skinny" in Spanish. The name is used extensively and indiscriminately in Peru.   If you're calling out to a skinny guy who is beneath you socially, you might yell, "Hey *Flaco*."   It's also a common nickname that gets stuck to thin people.   This particular Flaco fit his name.   He was very tall and thin to gauntness.   His cheekbones were high and they shadowed sunken cheeks. His eyes were deep brown, deep set and startlingly intense. His hair was black and straight, in sharp contrast to the pale color of his skin. If Indian blood ran in him, it ran only a trickle.   All in all, he was a very handsome, somewhat tragic-looking figure.   He was probably about 25 then.   Flaco spoke perfect English, because he had lived in Huntington Beach, California for about ten years.   He was friendly and far from threatening.   There was a kind, an almost innocent look about him.   I declined his killer bud and his pure coke, but I asked him if he knew of a good bar in town.

"Absolutely. Best in town. Hundred percent. That's where I work. I just got off, but I'll escort you back there."

Escort? I'm thinking. Escort? Nobody says "escort" around these parts.

So we walked up the street about a block and a half to a place called Moma Oclo's Bar. Now considering that the original Moma Oclo was the wife of the first king, Manco Inca, and was revered as a demigoddess, I hoped the bar would be something special. It wasn't, but it was open at least, and there were a few people inside, and I hadn't found anything else and I didn't want to disappoint Flaco, so I decided to give it a try. I thanked him and turned to enter.

Flaco asks if he can join me. I hesitate for a moment. Do I really want to be seen hanging out with a known drug-dealer? Then I look at him, look at this innocent face with its trace of anxiety, and I say sure. But I'm not entirely comfortable with the idea.

We sit at the bar and I order a Pisco Sour, the national cocktail of Peru. He doesn't order anything. I look at him and say, "Aren't you drinking?"

"I'm too broke," he says. I'm trying to save my money to go to school.

"What kind of school?" I ask.

"Tourism. I want to become a guide."

Considering that he was broke, I figured he wasn't all that successful as a drug dealer and was probably wise to think about school. I didn't know at the time just how right I was.

I took a few sips of my Pisco Sour. It's a pleasant drink, made with Pisco, which is a grape distillate of sugar, lemon and whipped egg white. The concoction was fine, but I couldn't enjoy it while

Flaco was sitting there with nothing to drink. I'm feeling sorry for him. I look at him and he is already looking at me and I can see the question coming, so I beat him to it.

"Can I buy you a drink?"

He lights up. "Thanks Richard. You're a prince." He orders a beer and a shot of the most expensive tequila in the house. Nothing shy about this Flaco. But what the hell, I think. You've got to expect it. Compared to this boy, I am rich, and he knows it.

Flaco senses the softie in me and rises to the occasion. One beer and tequila is followed by another, then another, and I keep up with him, so that after a couple of hours we are pretty drunk. Flaco turns out to be a good drinking partner. We talk about the Incas and their history. We talk about the girls of Peru. We even talk about literature, if you can believe it. Flaco tells me one of his favorite authors is Aldous Huxley. This stuns me. I read most of Huxley's novels when I was about nineteen and he was one of the writers who had spurred my interest in literature. "Which books of his have you read?" I ask him. And right off he says, "Eyeless in Gaza," and begins to tell me some of the plot. This is oddly serendipitous. I had recently been trying to remember the names of those Huxley novels that had so inspired me. And here was this kid, this Peruvian, this woefully indiscreet and unsuccessful drug dealer, taking me back to thoughts lost for forty years. Whatever his faults, I'm beginning to like the guy. There's something sort of rounded about a bad drug dealer who's read Huxley. We end up closing the bar.

I go to my hotel and Flaco goes wherever it is that he goes. The next day I go to Machu Picchu, and that, I assume, is the end of Flaco.

*   *   *   *

No such luck. About six months later I'm back home in the USA and I get a collect call from Flaco. He's coming to the states and wants to know if I know anybody who'd like to buy some coke in quantity.

He comes right out with this on the phone on an international call, a collect international call! I can't believe this guy. I can't believe he's not in jail. He talks about drugs as if it were soap or cereal. I tell him I'm not interested and ask him how he got my telephone number.

"You gave me your card."

There you go. Just like me. "Well don't call me collect any more," I say. "Okay, Flaco? Especially with that kind of talk"

"Yeah, yeah. I'm sorry Richard. I won't do it again."

And he didn't. At least he didn't call me collect with a drug deal again.

*　　*　　*　　*

Now it's a year and a half since I first encountered Flaco, and I am in Cusco for a month. I have just come from an exhibit of black and white photographs by Martin Chambi. In the twenties and thirties this man recorded the people and scenery of Cusco and its environs. It is fascinating to see Machu Picchu still partly covered with vegetation, to see Cusco as it was before the airport and the tourists. The photos are wonderfully luminous, especially a self-portrait of Chambi examining one of his photographs. The images have the detail that can only come from a big negative. It must have been hard work, for his tool was a huge 8 x 10 camera, which is on display along with his photographs.

I'm headed for the plaza and I hear a voice behind me calling my name.

"Richard. Richard Nisbet!"

Who in this town knows my last name, I wonder. Very few, but Flaco apparently, is one of them. He comes up smiling and gives me a good firm handshake. We talk for a few minutes and then he tells me he's gotten married and has a baby.

"That's wonderful!" I slap him on the back. "Congratulations."

Then his expression grows doleful. "Listen, Richard, I'm desperate. I'm starting a job next week, but my baby needs some medicine and I don't have money for it."

The perfect approach for old Just-Fell-Off-The-Turnip-Truck Richard. I lend him 50 sols on the condition that he never asks to borrow money from me again.

Flaco throws his arms around me. "You're a prince, Richard. You're a God."

Prince to God. That's a pretty good raise for the equivalent of $14.28, U.S.

A few days later I pass him and some of his friends on the plaza. He runs over, hugs me and says to his friends, "This guy is a prince. He saved my life. Only a couple of days and I am already demoted from God back down to Prince. How quickly they forget.

Flaco starts showing up at one of the bars I frequent. One day he has a few bucks and buys me a drink. He makes a big deal out of it. It's easy to tell when Flaco has, or recently had, something to sell. It's easy, because he burns or snorts up a goodly part of his supply, and gets this wild-eyed look and loses whatever little caution he ever had. He sits beside me at a crowded bar and says, "Richard, I have this killer weed. No seeds, no shake, just pure bud."

I wouldn't mind having some grass, but there is a man of the cloth sitting beside me. I glare at Flaco and growl, "I'm not interested,"

He gives me a strange look with his wild eyes. "Okay," he says.

Later I see him on my way out of the bathroom. "Are you crazy Flaco? Don't you EVER approach me like that in front of other people."

He hangs his head like a bad little boy caught raiding the cookie jar.. "I'm sorry, Richard. I won't do it again."

A week later I see him in the same bar. I'm talking to some reasonably respectable-looking gringos and Flaco comes up to me and says, "Can I see you outside for a minute, Richard?"

"In a minute," I say. I go on talking to the gringos for a while, then excuse myself. Flaco is waiting by the bathroom. "Are you crazy Flaco? Don't you EVER approach me like that in front of other people. For God's sake, if you're going to be a drug dealer, take some lessons, go to school. You're terrible."

Flaco hangs his head and says, "I'm sorry Richard. I won't do it again."

He didn't do that one again, but he kept showing up at the bar and trying to get me to buy him drinks. Sometimes I did, sometimes I didn't. One day he shows up bruised and disheveled and feistier than ever. "I just got out of jail," he says. "They arrested me for creating a disturbance."

"What kind of disturbance?" I ask.

He ignores the question. "But I showed them. I said 'Fuck you, you stupid cops, what do you know? You don't know jack."

"And what did they do?"

"They beat the shit out of me."

"And then what?"

"They let me go." He caressed one of his wounds. "Vigilante justice. I told them they were a bunch of asshole pigs."

Oh, Flaco, I think, you are truly one of the worst drug dealers I have ever seen. I cannot imagine why you are not behind bars.

A week or so later he tells me that he's been banned from one of the other bars for creating a disturbance. Flaco seems to be going downhill faster than a bobsled on a straightaway.

*   *   *   *

One day this guy named John, shows up at the bar. John is in his fifties and has the air of experience wrapped about him. He's very self-possessed, self-assured. He is quiet and he doesn't smile a lot. He just sits by himself and nurses his drink and watches. I usually carry this little digital camera with me and use it as a way to connect with people. I'll go up to almost anyone and ask to take their picture. Then I show it to them on the little display and pretty soon we're friends and I have their email addresses so that I can send them a photo. I noticed right off that John seemed a little nervous about my camera. He never looks at me without shifting his gaze to it like it was the enemy.

Maybe it's the third time I've seen him and I go to his table and say, "Don't worry about the camera. I won't take your picture without asking." John just glares at me. I had hoped for better. I nod, walk away and leave him alone from then on.

After John has been there for a few days, Flaco comes in.

He's wearing his wild-eyes for sure. He sits at the bar, starts chattering, and tries to scam a drink. I remind him that the fifty sols I gave him was the last he'd get out of me.   He hangs his head for a moment, the looks up and orders an Inca Cola. I can't stand it. After all, he did buy a drink for me a while back. "Okay," I say, "I'll buy you a drink, but this is absolutely the last time. Got it?"

"Thanks Richard. You're a prince."

After we drink for a while, he notices John and asks about him.

"I don't know. He's not very friendly."

"He looks like he needs some blow."

"Don't even think about it, Flaco. The guy's weird. He could even be DEA."

"I don't think so. I know his type."

Flaco is on a tear and nothing is going to stop him. He takes the drink I bought him, goes over to John's table and sits down like he was invited.   It's easy to see that John is not the least interested in dealing with Flaco, but Flaco doesn't seem to care. They talk quietly for a few minutes. My ears are perked up. I hear Flaco say something about mother-of-pearl, and then John reaches across the table and slaps him hard in the face.   He hisses at Flaco, "You're ridiculous, boy. If you're going to be a drug dealer, for God's sake learn how to be a good one." Flaco hangs his head and I think I hear him mutter, "I'm sorry John."

After that, Flaco never tries to sell me drugs again.   Neither does he ask me to buy him drinks. He doesn't need to. For five days in a row, he and John sit together in a corner table in intense, *sotto voce* conversation. John is buying the drinks.

And then they are gone. Both of them.

A week later, I go back to the states.

*   *   *   *

Six months later I am back in Cusco and within hours I run into Flaco. He looks different. He looks like he doesn't have money worries. It's not that he is dressed better or is wearing a Rolex or ringed with 24 carat gold chains. He just seems more relaxed and self-confident.

"You're looking good, Flaco."

"Thanks, Richard. I'm feeling good."

"How's your wife and baby?"

"They're great. They're at the house." He pauses for effect. "Oh, I bought a house here in Cusco. Out in Larrapa. It's where the money is going. The best people are building out there: doctors, lawyers, politicians…"

I'm beginning to get the idea. "That's great, Flaco. I'm happy for you. What're you doing these days?"

He gives me an innocent smile. "Oh this and that." Then he pats me on the back "By the way, I owe you some money, don't I?"

"Fifty Sols," I say.

Flaco reaches into his pocket and pulls out a wad of money. The wad isn't Sols, it's U.S. dollars. He riffles through it and pulls out a fifty-dollar bill.

"Here y'go."

"But Flaco, you owe me fifty sols, not fifty dollars."

"Interest," he says. He slaps me on the back again. "And I owe you a few drinks, too. Gotta go now, but I'll see you at the bar."

Then he does something very strange. Something I've never seen, even from soldiers, in Peru. He does a military about face, looks back at me with a wink and walks off, standing tall.

*   *   *   *

I have this sneaking suspicion that Flaco went to school.

POPCORN BOY

It was a maybe a year and a half ago when I first en-countered the little guy we began to call "Popcorn Boy." He showed up at Duffy's Place with a bag of popcorn and a simple, expressionless face, a face devoid of guile, a face so full of innocence that most prudent folks would have suspected something other than face value.

But I am a classic, cockeyed optimist. Not only that, I love popcorn. My dentist tells me it's horrible for my teeth, but it seems to be good for my gut and my spirit and so far hasn't done damage to my dental apparatus... the original or the improved. Before popcorn boy appeared, I used to walk several blocks down *Avenida del Sol* to buy it from an old fellow who had a cart with a gas fired popper and sold the stuff at the price of one sol for a pitifully small bag. It was good popcorn. It tasted like the kind you buy in movie theatres in the states, the stuff that tastes so good because it is made with copious amounts of artery-clogging coconut oil.

But then popcorn boy entered the scene and I started buying from him. The popcorn wasn't quite as good as the old man's, but it seemed healthier and it was, so to speak, delivered. The little guy began to come around regularly to Duffy's. He would stand there, all three and a half feet of him, and with that irresistible face of his he would extend a plastic-wrapped tube-bag of popcorn. No promo, no hype. Usually the kid street vendors have this horrible technique, learned I-don't-know-where that consists of persistent and horrible whining. *Amigo..... Amiigooo... buy from me... why you no buy from me Amigo?* And so on until you're about ready to throttle the little buggars. I have more than once tried to evade them by getting on the other side of a street, a wall, a gaggle of tourists, or even, in direst circumstances, an automobile. This, I think, is why I became partial to Popcorn Boy. He didn't whine or beg, he simply offered. And always that face that could melt you, and, directed properly, could make a pile of money at a poker table. I always accepted that which Popcorn Boy offered.

I left Cusco to return to the States for a couple of months. Popcorn boy, I was told, continued to show up at Duffy's, no doubt filled with disappointment over my absence. After a while Duffy's began to refuse him entrance. I suppose the feeling was that he was diminishing the Frito sales. Person-ally I thought the popcorn was increasing the beverage sales, but then I don't run the place, I just spend a lot of time there.

Part of the Cusco scene is the repeated attempts of street vendors, children, usually, to get into restaurants and bars and sell their chewing gum, candy, cigarettes.... and popcorn. They dart in quietly and pester the customers until the they are ushered out, sometimes rudely, sometimes kindly, by an owner or a waiter. It's a game of survival for both of them. Just think about it. One of them sleeps on a dirt floor with the other members of a large family who wear ragged clothes and eat rice and potatoes, and the other is trying to entice tourists, who don't want a bunch of ragged kids begging while they are eating. I understand where both sides are coming from.

Two months later when I returned to Cusco a the popcorn scene had mushroomed...or popcorned. I got the feeling that Popcorn Boy and I had started something. Street popcorn vendors seemed to be everywhere now. Of course my supplier Popcorn Boy was still there as well. But there was a difference. Popcorn Boy charged one sol for his bag of canchitas. The others were selling their same-sized bag for half a sol. The others also whined and begged in the time-honored fashion.

One time my friend Paul read Popcorn Boy the riot act for bilking the tourists. "Go home and tell your mother that your price is unfair and it gives Cusco a bad name." Personally, I don't care. The difference is 50 centimos, which at this time amounted to about fourteen cents US. This is nothing. Once I told him that everybody else was charging only a half-sol and he agreed to take that. I gave him the full sol anyway. After all, we are in collusion. Popcorn Boy and I have injected something new into the Cusco scene. Together we are pioneers. I gladly pay his price. *The fourteen cents ees nothing!*

Before I go on, a few words about popcorn and the Spanish language. Popcorn in Spanish is "*Palomitas de mais.*" "*Paloma*" in Spanish is "dove." Corn is "*Mais.*" "*Palomita*" is "little dove". Popped corn looks like a little dove.

Simple enough, yes? But it goes on. The colloquial hereabouts for popcorn is "*canchitas.*" *Canchitas* is much easier to get out of your mouth than "*palomitas de mais.*" But using the colloquial is fraught with danger. Here's why: *Concha* in Spanish is a cognate. It's a conch shell. "*Conchita*" is colloquial for "pussy," and I am not referring to the small cat kind. So if you slip up and ask for "*conchitas*" rather than "*canchitas*" you get giggles and smirks. Consequently, I must pause before asking for, referring to, or offering popcorn here in Cusco.

Now back to Popcorn Boy. From the very beginning, he has had an unerring ability to track me. He'll sneak into Duffy's, stand where only I can see him, and proffer his bag. He never says anything, he just holds out that bag of popcorn. When I began to spend some of my time at Rosie O'Grady's, he tracked me there. I would look up from my reading to see that mutely extended bag of *canchitas*... Popcorn Boy behind it. I suppose if he knew my California address, he would still find me and I would get home delivery.

In the street, and in the street only, Popcorn Boy actually opens his mouth and speaks. More than once he has come up behind me, his voice proceeding him with the simple word *"canchitas?"*

One night, en route to Rosie O'Grady's, I hear behind me the treasured word. I stop, turn and face none other than the original, my friend and supplier, Popcorn Boy. I smile and agree to purchase. Popcorn boy does not smile. I have never seen popcorn boy smile. He doesn't scowl or frown or show any expression at all. He is angelic and uncluttered in his mien.

I reach for money and find not quite enough in change for a one-sol bag. Popcorn boy assures me he has change for a ten sol note. He digs in his pocket but comes up short. This does not stop him, though. No, sir, no way does it stop my man, the original. He leaves me standing on the street with my tube of popcorn in hand, leaves his fabric bag containing his complete inventory lying on the sidewalk and he dashes across the street to the Amadeus Bar & Grille. He disappears inside for two or three seconds then dashes out, runs farther down the street to the Kathmandu Bar & Grille where the same scene is repeated. On down the street he runs, darting into one *tienda* after another to beg for change. On the fourth attempt he succeeds. He comes flying back to me, change in hand, artfully dodging the taxis, whose drivers, every one of them, seem to think they are in a *grand prix* road race.

All this took about two minutes. He gives me my change. I am so astonished at this performance that I decide to escalate our relationship. I do something I've never done before. I ask his name.

"Miguel," he says, in a very small voice.

"Ricardo," I say and shake his hand. His grip is tentative, his eyes are averted.

There is still no smile, there is still that innocent, expressionless face that is so irresistible.

But something momentous has happened. We, who have together instigated the distribution of popcorn in Cusco, are no longer nameless.

I am no longer just the white-haired gringo who loves canchitas. I am Ricardo.

And Popcorn Boy is now Miguel.

*I'll tell you, it makes me feel good. I begin to have these fantasies. I can see Miguel a few years from now. He'll have a little cart and he'll be selling popcorn in many flavors and the people will go nuts over it and after a few more years he'll be packing the stuff in designer containers and it'll be **POPCORN BOY POPCORN**. Or maybe **POPCORN BOY CANCHITAS**, I don't know. But I do know I believe in the kid and want him to succeed.*

Later I begin to wonder. It's been six months and I've been out of, and back into, Cusco and everything's changed again. Now the popcorn vendors seem to have disappeared. I can't believe this! Was popcorn simply a fad? Are my friend and I victims of a flash-in-the-pan market? I don't see Popcorn Boy all the thirty days I'm here and I fret about his health, both physical and economic.

Now here's a lesson. This is August/September, their planting time. I don't think about the season having any effect on markets. For God's sake, Orville Redenbacher and Jiffy Pop are buying up popping corn on the Chicago commodities exchange. *They don't have to worry about seasons.* But apparently they do here in the Andes.

It was not always so. Before their civilization was wrecked by the Spanish, the Incas were very big on storage. All over this part of the Andes you see ruins of granaries high on the slopes of hills where the enemy would have a beast of a time stealing food. The Incas not only protected themselves from theft, they protected themselves from nature's theft... from those sure-to-come-along lean years.

Popcorn Boy, of course, has no such insurance. The corn is harvested in March/April, the Austral Fall, and by the Austral Spring it's all damn near gone and planting is underway.

I go and come again and I am here in the Austral summer and once more the popcorn business is flourishing. I see plenty of vendors, but for a long time, there is no evidence of Popcorn Boy... Miguel. I hope and I worry. I hope that my pard has made so much money that he is studying investment banking. On the other hand I worry that somehow he might have priced himself out of the market with his exorbitant price.

Maybe Paul was right. Oh, my Popcorn Boy, my Miguel, I hope you have been charging your other customers the going price of only fifty centimos per bag. and not the full sol you charge me.

But finally, thankfully, my man showed up. He had changed. He had diversified. He had the familiar old basket of popcorn over one shoulder. But across the other, hanging along his back, was a shoeshine kit. Shocking. It appeared that Popcorn Boy had joined the gang of about six thousand Cusco shoeshine boys.

I don't like this. I don't like this at all. Shoeshine boys are the town's absolutely worst hustlers. They are the worst hustlers in all of Peru. They drive me nuts. And lest I seem insensitive and politically incorrect, let me explain just why with this little scenario:

SHOESHINE BOY: Shoeshine?

(or, if they've seen you around for more than two days)

SHOESHINE BOY: Amigo! Remember me? Shoeshine? Only one sol, Amigo. Special!

It's that "special" that really pisses me off. Follow this:

SHOESHINE BOY: (After the Gringo has agreed to his one sol price... working furiously on the shoes and chattering all the time, pulls out a bottle of something unrecognizable and shakes it at you) Special! Special!

The Gringo Customer, who has no idea what the kid is saying, gives a non-committal shrug. The process continues until both shoes have received the "special" treatment.

SHOESHINE BOY: Five Sols.

GRINGO: *Five Sols! You said ONE sol.*

SHOESHINE BOY: For Special. Five Sols.

There you go. I bought it one time and that was enough. Once in Pisac I refused to buckle to this worn-out coercion and the kid persisted. He carried on and on, and finally he was beating himself on the head with his shoeshine brush. Not being anywhere near wanting to encourage such weird behavior, I called the waiter and told him to banish the jerk so I could eat in peace.

So you can see why I hated to see my man join those ranks. For one thing, it seemed to be a step down the ladder, and for another, Popcorn Boy didn't have the brass, the push and the deviousness to compete in the shoeshine arena.

Miguel, of course, has no idea what hopes I hold for him. There's something steady and open and honest about him and I think it is just what is needed in this clutch of whining, pleading street merchants of the Andes.

There was something else different now about Popcorn Boy. Pubescence was creeping up on him. He had lost part of that total innocence. Miguel was sliding into the transitional age, and although he still had all his familiar and comforting reticence, he was a little less a child.

I felt a downward tug of despair.

I kept seeing Popcorn boy. He still stalked me at Duffy's. In deference to Duff, I would tell Miguel I wasn't interested today. Then I would follow him out the door and buy... buy like a drug addict, lurking in the shadows to make the deal.

One night Duff and I are leaving his bar to go to Ukuku's Disco to listen to a guitarist we both like. We're almost out the door when Popcorn Boy enters. He's got his basket of popcorn, but he's dumped the shoeshine kit. I told him I wasn't interested tonight. Duffy detours for some reason and I walk outside with Miguel.

"Okay," I say. "I'll buy a bag." Duff's not looking.

Miguel hands me the bag and I hand him a one-sol piece. He looks at me with that face, hands the coin back to me and says, "But I owe you a sol."

"What?" I say, but then I begin to remember.

"The last time you only had a two sol piece and I didn't have change. You said I owed you."

I was stunned. Simply stunned. I thought about all the hustlers, the whiners and the near-thieves I've encountered in this country... and I damn near wept.

My Man. My Popcorn Boy. My Miguel... He was standing tall.

I gave him the sol back. *"Una propina...* a tip."

I patted him on the shoulder. "Gracias, Miguel."

And he, with his still pre-adolescent voice, replies, "Gracias Reechar."

Later I told Duffy about this salubrious event. His facial expression evidenced mild approval. Then for the first time he explained to my why he didn't want Popcorn Boy or any other kids coming in to his bar to sell their goods. "It's because they're children," he said. "Why are the parents sending their kids out into the street to work while they sit on their asses at home? It's not right."

"How do you know the parents aren't out working themselves?"

"Well, I'll bet most of them aren't."

Maybe so, maybe no. But I think of the fact that a day of manual labor here earns only 15 to 20 sols and I can see where a parent might be coming from asking his kids to get out there and earn a little something.

On the other hand, lately there seem to be a lot of five year olds out in the Plaza hustling tourists late into the night. That doesn't seem right.

I'm withholding judgment.

And I'm still buying popcorn from Miguel. As evidence of our new credit relationship, there is usually a small float between us. He might owe me a sol or a half-sol, or it might be the other way around. I let him keep the books.

I'm also teaching him how to shake hands with a firm grip and to look you in the eye when he does. He's having problem looking me in the eye, but he always shakes hands. He even reminds me if I forget.

Duffy continued to make every effort to keep Miguel out of his bar, but he was fighting a losing battle. Other customers, and even some of the staff, began to surreptitiously work on the little guy's behalf.

For example:

I am talking to a friend at the bar. Suddenly she isn't listening to me. She casts her eyes left and nods her head slightly in the same direction. I give her a curious look. She repeats, and I finally get it and look. A bag of popcorn peeks around the corner. I hustle over and sneak in a transaction with Miguel.

The staff took to keeping him at the entrance, then coming to me and whispering, "*Popcorn Boy.*" Once, when I didn't get to him fast enough, one of the staff and one of the customers ran out the door and down the steps, chased down Miguel and returned with two bags. He only charged them a sol for the two bags. If you think this makes me angry, you are wrong. You know I delight in paying twice the going price. It's a very small investment in Popcorn Boy's future.

The war goes on. I try to buy now from Miguel in the street before I come in to the bar. Once, when I pulled it out of my daypack, Duffy looks and asks, "Where'd you get that?"

"Popcorn Boy," I say.

"Contraband," says Duff. He gives me a stern, disapproving look.

Then, lips still drawn taught near to snapping, he reaches a hand across the bar and says,

"Gimmie some."

WILFREDO

"Tu unica problema es tu cara." Your only problem is your face. It's a phrase I learned from a Bolivian friend that I like to throw at Wilfredo every now and then.

Wilfredo is a barman at Duffy's Place. He has the kind of good looks that modeling agencies in the U.S. look for. He'd have to do something about all that Peruvian gold in his teeth, but otherwise he's GQ cover material.

Wilfredo has a lively spirit. His laugh is frequent and easy and it always comes in couplets: Ha-HA! In reality Wilfredo's laugh seems more a punctuation. Ha-HA! He has another couplet greeting. It's a clicking sound he makes with his tongue that comes out of the side of his mouth. Clk-CLK. I walk into the bar and Wilfredo grins and greets me. Clk-CLK!

I'm trying to teach Wilfredo the little magic I know. It's not much of a gift because I know even less magic than I know Spanish. But I think he has a knack for it, and I don't think there is one single magician in Cusco. Teach a man to fish......

Wilfredo's English is skimpier than my Spanish, but we manage somehow, always trying to teach each other our native tongues. One day he tells me that he wants me to come to his place for lunch, which his wife will prepare. I am surprised to discover he has a wife. Wilfredo is so good looking that I thought he might be gay. His wife he says, is 18 and he is 23 and she is expecting a child in a few weeks.

Before we set a date, he adds Jim to the guest list. Jim is a Minnesota gringo, a Peruvian sweater exporter and my good friend. Jim has spent more time down here than I have and his Spanish is vastly superior to mine, so I'm glad to have him along to help me penetrate the linguistic intricacies of the language.

On the appointed day, Wilfredo comes down to meet Jim and me at my apartment. This is necessary because, as we later discovered, we could never have found his home without help. We hail a taxi. There is haggling over the price with Jim refusing to pay more than 3 sols. The driver doesn't like it, but he acquiesces... at least for the moment. We slice our way through the customarily insane Cusco traffic and begin climbing the hill of Carmenca. We are held up for five or ten minutes by the train to Machu Picchu, which, for some reason is stopped and blocking our way. There have been rumors of landslides and we surmise that this is connected. But finally the train passes and we are able to cross the tracks and continue our ascent. At the peak of the hill there is a brace of antennas and satellite dishes. I remember reading that where the antennas now stand there used to be three stone towers erected by the Incas to mark the passage of the sun and the times for planting in various altitudes. The Spanish, of course, had no use for such idolatry and hastened to raze the towers.

Near the top of the hill, Wilfredo tells the driver to stop. There is another argument about money. We give him more than the agreed amount, but the driver goes away unhappy anyway.

I take a few moments to look down into the valley. The sky is gray and the air is misty, but still, the view from here is remarkable and it makes manifest the history of this city. To the right and the left are the two lifelines that are rescuing Cusco from the decrepit, stinking, nearly forgotten backwater it had become in the centuries since the Spanish had moved the seat of power to Lima.

To the far right the airport jet runway is like an arrow pointing deeper into the valley. Below and to the left the tracks of the Machu Picchu narrow-gauge railway curl in and out of sight. Between these two essentials is the city of Cusco, visible from this elevated vantage point mostly as red tiled roofs with patches of whitewashed walls beneath. To the left of the city rises the hill of San Cristobal and at the top, the ruins, the mighty stone walls that remain of the fortress/ temple/storehouse/ reservoir/redoubt, Sacsahuaman. Just below us the land slopes down beyond the tracks. It is spotted with adobe dwellings, unwhitewashed deep red walls topped with lighter red tiles. All around are green hills hueing to blue in the distance.

We are standing above the gorge carved by the Huatanay River. On the other side of the hill of Sacsahuaman the land dips again into the gorge carved by the Tullumayu River. Somewhere down near the airport the two rivers converge. The rivers are now covered by streets and buildings but once they, along with the walls of Sacsahuaman, must have offered some measure of protection against enemies.

Behind us the hill of Carmenca continues to rise. Wilfredo lives up there somewhere. We begin to climb the few hundred feet to his place. There is no real path, so we scamper from level to level. Above us are scattered numerous adobe dwellings. We come to Wilfredo's home, a simple building with three or four doors and an equal number of small windows. He opens his door and ushers us into his home.

His wife is there to welcome us. She is short and round and pretty and looks to be more like 14 than 18. A table is set for four in the middle of the small space that is their dining room. A curtain hangs to one side to separate the single room into sleeping and eating areas. The walls are a hideous lime green and the light comes from a single florescent tube that only makes the walls more ghastly. It is reminiscent of county lockups. Through a window we get a glimpse of what we later discover is a communal kitchen. Several women are tending the wood fired stove and now and then Wilfredo's wife goes out to help with the cooking. I wonder just what degree of neighborly input is involved here.

It begins to rain, softly at first, then hard. My first concern is getting back down he hill in the mud, without a staff, on my bum legs. Wilfredo assures me it won't be a problem. He then proceeds to show us the rest of his home. He pulls back the curtain and we enter the bedroom. There is, of course, a double bed, and in contrast to the simplicity of everything else about this home, there is a television and two boom boxes. One is old, the other new and silver-shiny. Wilfredo tells us he saved his pennies for two years to buy it. The cost was equivalent to about three months of his wages. The rent for his room is 50 sols per month, about a tenth of his salary.

When the meal is ready we sit to eat. There is salad of tomato and onion, *choclos*, their corn with the huge kernels, two varieties of potatoes and the local trout, which is pink like salmon and delicious.

There is little conversation. Wilfredo's wife is shy and only speaks when spoken to. We find that they both come from the district of Apurimac, named after the river that flows through it. Apurimac means "great speaker" in Quechua. The river roars through deep and precipitous gorges. I remember reading about the rope bridge over the Apurimac, about the trepidation of the Spanish horses crossing the bridge, about the destruction of it during one of the battles of Manco Inca's rebellion.

After we finish our meal, Wilfredo brings out a 2 1/4-liter bottle of Coca Cola and opens it as though it were a bottle of fine wine. We drink and toast, and then it is time to leave. We thank Wilfredo's wife and part with the customary kiss to the cheek.

The rain has let up somewhat, but the slope is slippery now... Wilfredo offers a hand and I gladly accept. We wait at the road for a taxi. If no taxi comes, we'll settle for a combi, which is a van designed to hold nine passengers but always seems to be carrying fifteen or twenty. The rain increases. Several taxis pass us, but they are in service. Finally comes a combi with reasonable room for Jim and me.

Wilfredo waves goodbye and starts back up the hill to his home.

I am preoccupied with thoughts of this young couple and what a struggle their life is. I feel almost ashamed of my relative wealth. A lump rises to my throat and I determine to do something for them.

A few weeks later someone repaid $100 that I had lent them three months before. That night, in the bar, I called Wilfredo over and laid the $100 bill down under my hand with these words: "Don't tell anybody about his except for your wife. This is only for your baby."

I shoved the hundred over to him. He covered it and bowed his head. There were tears in his eyes as there were in mine when I left his house that day.

"Thank you, Richar."

All the next day I pondered this exchange, and pondered the nature of giving.

"What a fine guy I am," I think momentarily. "I've given him what would take him nearly a month to earn."

But then I check myself, Who are you doing this for? Are you doing this to make yourself feel like a big shot? Or is it really for him and his wife.

I don't want to approach Wilfredo with the attitude that gratitude is expected. I want to be cool about it.

When I walk in the next night, Wilfredo acts as though he has divined my thoughts. He greets me with his couplet clicks.

And then there is the briefest movement of his hand to his heart.

No more is said then or later.

That was enough.

* * * *

A few weeks later Wilfredo was fired. He brought it on himself. He was unhappy with the job and he repeatedly failed to show up for work. Jim and I begged Duff not to fire him, but Duff has a business to run and he would not relent.

Now we keep an eye out, Jim & I, for help wanted signs... and for Wilfredo, so that we can tell him about this or that opportunity. But it's been days now and there has been no sign of the boy.

I suspect that he may have gone back to Apurimac with his wife and the child that will soon be with us.

Cusco can be a tough town.

* * * *

About a year has passed now, and I am happy to report that I was wrong about Wilfredo's fate. He hung on here in Cusco. His daughter is now about eight months old.

I first encountered him in Gringo Alley. He was looking just fine. He was wearing his old smile and a clean white shirt. He was on the street trying to hustle clients into a restaurant that was on the second floor. I went in once. I had been there before. It was an okay place.

Next time I saw Wilfredo he was out on the street hustling clients for his own restaurant. He was a partner in the new Wasi Grill. He looked so fine. I had already had dinner but I promised him I would come back the next day. I did, and ate a very nice meal on a table with a white tablecloth.

I took a picture of Wilfredo.

Remember... Wasi Grill on Procuradores. Otherwise known as Gringo Alley. It's on the left about a third of the way up. Tell 'em Richard sent you.

HAPPY HOUR

This is my ordeal as I traverse the five blocks from my apartment to Rosie O'Grady's for the 6:00 to 7:00 P.M. happy hour, which, unfortunately coincides with the Cusco rush hour.

Casoleta Recoleta, the small collection of apartments wherein I am living, is nestled within a safe, enclosed space. It is a little oasis of renovation, tasteful decoration, flowers and grass. But open the blue door that gates the little complex and the reality of Cusco strikes.

Just beyond the 21-inch sidewalk is Calle Recoleta, which to my knowledge is the narrowest street in Cusco that permits vehicular traffic. Calle Recoleta is a one-way street for the simple and obvious reason that no two cars could possibly pass each other.

On my side of the street the sidewalk ranges in width from about 21 to 14 inches. The narrowest section is flanked by a wall that leans in to the street, so that you must walk slopingly, like someone with a horrible spinal affliction. The other side of the street ranges from 21 inches to nothing with nothing predominating, so that it is only useful in certain situations, which I will soon describe.

My course will take me to the left so that I am walking against both vehicular and pedestrian traffic. To step into the street is folly. The cars and busses rocket through fiercely, and only if the car is a Daewoo Tico (A swollen 4 passenger roller skate that has never been seen on the broad streets and avenues of North America) is there room for a person *and* a car. And even in that case, the pedestrian is at high risk.

I take a few tentative steps down the sidewalk and am met with a phalanx of pedestrians. Backs against the wall, we wait for a break in the traffic. A Tico passes and two courageous little boys dart into the street and pass me. Seconds later there is a break and we opposing pedestrians step into the street and nearly collide. A bus is bearing down upon us so we all quickly jump back onto the sidewalk. Now there is a fairly long break in the traffic. I can see a Toyota taxi entering the eye of the needle perhaps 150 feet down the street. All pedestrians are moving against my direction. My eyes dart quickly to the opposite side of the street, my mind calculating furiously. There is a short space of usable sidewalk there that will take me another fifteen feet down the road until I must cross back to my side to continue. I cross the street and proceed. But by the time I come to the no-sidewalk part, the cars are racing down Calle Recoleta like a hurtling train. I press my back against the wall and pray. Outside rearview mirrors slice the air within inches of my vulnerable body.

Finally there is another break. I get across the street and carefully negotiate another few yards before being met by more oncoming cars and pedestrians. We all squeeze ourselves back against he wall. We look at each other to attempt some silent agreement as to who will step into the street at the next break in traffic. I try to be the gentlemen with the old and infirm and make that dangerous move myself, but often as not we both do the same and then have to dodge each other as well as the traffic.

I am coming close to the end of the street where it widens and changes its name from Calle Recoleta to Calle Siete Ventanas. Just as the street widens, a stairway descends to my left. There is no sidewalk for a few feet here, only street and a little raised curb about 10 inches wide. Unless there is no traffic, I must walk this curb like a tightrope, knowing that a slip will take me either into an onrushing taxi or down about thirty stone steps.

Past this, a vendor's cart forces me to either take to the street or the muddy passageway to its left. Beyond the vendor's cart a car is typically parked half on the street and half on the sidewalk. If I take the left route, I am often as not blocked by a little boy pissing against the wall. If I take the right, I must deal with the onrushing traffic. But once past these obstacles I enter the relative broadness of Siete Ventanas where there is room for two-way pedestrian traffic. I heave a sigh of relief. I have safely made it through the eye of the needle.

On to the next challenge. Now the street curves around to the left and becomes Santa Catalina Ancha. Most evenings, an old Indian woman squats before her kerosene stove cooking potatoes and corn and *anticuchos*, (brochette in your better restaurants, meat-on-a-stick on the street). It smells enticing, but I have time restraints. Happy hour ends in a few minutes.

Just past, on the left is Calle Tullumayo. It rises up a steep hill and enters Santa Catalina. There are stop signs here, but no one pays them the least attention. The traffic is furious. This is, I think, the location of Cusco's most intense game of automobile chicken. Taxi's charge up the hill and into the middle of the intersection. How they decide who will pass and who will stop is a total mystery to me. They come within inches of each other before one relents and gives way. Strangely enough, there is no blowing of horns in this midst of this tangle. There is some tacit agreement regarding right of way. Even more strangely, I have never seen a collision here. Still I am filled with trepidation. Having been hit by a speeding car once in my life, I have little courage when crossing streets.

I spot a cluster of little old ladies and children who are looking for an opening in the traffic and I cling to them for protection. A traffic policeman stands on one of the corners, but for what reason, I cannot fathom. He rarely directs traffic and when he does, no thought is given to the poor pedestrians who have been waiting fearfully for so long to cross the street. Mostly what he does is blow his whistle whenever he needs to assert his presence. (I complained once to a local friend about the absurdity of all this and her response was, "Isn't it like that everywhere?")

Finally there is an opening in the traffic and we bustle across, myself hiding behind the skirts of the most decrepit old lady I can find.

The worst is now over. Two blocks lie between Rosie O'Grady's and me. I look at my watch. Happy hour is over in five minutes. There is only one more intersection and that one is relatively simple. I need only cross San Agustin where it enters Santa Catalina Ancha from my left. Usually there are not many vehicles on this street.

But tonight there is a disturbance. Traffic is stopped and scores of horns are raging. As I get closer I see that, in the middle of the intersection, two dogs are hung up after their love fest and another male is trying hopelessly to make it a canine *ménage a trois*. In the very middle of the intersection, the three horny hounds skitter, crablike, this way and that. My last obstacle, San Augustine is a solid line of taxis, stretching way down the hill.

It would seem a simple thing to just slide between two vehicles, but not so here. The drivers are all riding their clutches, lurching forward and sliding backward until scant inches are between them and the car behind. I can see my poor legs being crunched between a bus and a Toyota taxi. So I turn left and head down San Agustin, hoping to find the end of this line of lurching vehicles. I get there, cross the street and hurry up the other side. It is now two minutes before Rosie's happy hour ends. I walk in confidently, doing the glad-hand, all smiles, proffering handshakes and cheek kisses (always the right cheek). Then I look at the clock.

Either their clock is fast or mine is slow. The clock above the bar says 7:02.

Happy hour at a Rosie O'Grady's has ended.

Charlie, my friend who owns Rosie's, read this story and said in all sincerity, "But Richard, you know they would have served you a happy hour anyway."

"But Charlie," I said. "Where would that leave me for punch line?"

THE PROFESSOR

There are many who come to Cusco because they believe there is something highly spiritual about this part of the world. If you've ever watched the dawn come forth from the heights of Machu Picchu, seen the mist blossom and float up from the Urubamba River, been awed by the sheer precipitous rise of these mountains, you are likely to feel awed by the majesty and grace and beauty that exists here and there on our planet.

The Stones of Sacsahuaman are so huge, so intricately fitted that a whole cult believes that aliens built them. And a subchapter of that group also believes that the aliens will come on our New Year, land at Sacsahuaman and take us away to eternal bliss.

My approach is more mechanical. I have found no satisfactory explanation of how Stones of up to several hundred tons were dragged for miles, then cut and fitted together with an accuracy unequalled anywhere else on earth. It had been my aim on this trip to encounter an academic who might be able to enlighten me.

Today it happened.

My friends René and Yheni took me to see her professor. I was told that he had been studying the stoneworks for years and believed that they were 3-D maps of fundamental mathematical principals. He had been Yheni's professor at the University, and apparently the one she most admired. We climbed west of the Plaza de Armas, made our way up another of those streets that changes names every block, and came to a non-descript door that opened into its own enclosed world. This particular world had something to do with the university.   We came to a curtained doorway beyond which there was a lighted room.

Yheni, knocked. "Profi?" She spoke in that female voice that is reserved for loved ones of the opposite sex with whom a conjugal encounter is totally out of the question.   The knock and the oh so sweetly spoken "Profi?" were presently answered by Dr. Huilman Huascar Quispe, professor of physics and mathematics at the local university. I was prepared to dislike him. Yheni had told me that he didn't drink...all he did was sit in front of his computer and try to fathom the stones. I have a certain distrust of those who don't drink, but I loved this man from the moment I saw him.   "Profi" must be in his 70's. He was roundish and twinklish and had a broad closed-mouth grin that made you think of Popeye. I guessed him to be around 5'5" and a good 175 pounds. Later he told me he was pure Quechua, but I have my doubts.   His nose wasn't quite the right shape and his color seemed a bit too yellow.

In these days of rediscovering Quechua roots, of peeling back the onion layers of cultural obliteration and obfuscation that were so assiduously laid on by the Spaniards, it is advantageous to claim any vestige of Inca Ancestry.   Perhaps a time will come when the descendents of those invaders will evidence some sense of shame and try to make amends. They will hopefully be so overwhelmed with guilt that the Profis of the Andes will be given profitable bingo concessions.

His office was about 8 X 15 feet.   Profi sat at his computer. At one end of the room, stacked on a table, was a veritable wall of 1970s vintage stereo gear. Two stacks of speakers and between them a tower of amplifiers, graphic equalizers, turntables and audio casset-te players their brushed-aluminum faces gleaming. At the other end of the room was even more stereo gear: two additional pairs of speakers, and scraps of stereo and computer hardware.   This man was *wired*.   His huge collection of books occupied every remaining nook and cranny in this little room.

I had been given to understand that Profi was fluent in English, but such was hardly the case. As we sat down, gathering around his monitor for the show that was to come, we broached the matter of language. Profi asked me if I spoke Spanish. My reply was, "*Menos de poquito,*" which means damn nearly nothing. There was a good laugh all around, and Profi and I bonded on the spot. Thenceforth we each did our best with our silly syntax to break the language barrier. It was an unbelievably appropriate opening for what was to come later in our meeting.

Well," he said, once we had settled down, "What is it you want to know about the stones?"

Straightaway I answered with one word: "Why?"

His face, already alive, ratcheted ups another notch. He suggested that I might want to take notes, and I, ever the dutiful student, hauled out my Bic and my spiral-bound notebook and waited.

He began with a prepared presentation he had recently delivered before a conference of physicists in Chile. It was beautifully done with very nice, very simple animation. He even had a 3-D wire-frame graphic that he delighted in manipulating with the up-down-left-right arrows on his keyboard. He showed how Inca architecture could explain geometry in a way that was so much easier to understand than the formulae we use. He had scores of very nice photographs, many with overlaid outlines that faded in and out.

And finally he showed how an Inca vase was a perfect expression of a fractal. I am not overwhelmed with this thinking. Physical reality *is* fractals, and mathematics is an effort to explain physical reality.

For example, that business of Pi appearing in the dimensions of the great pyramid even though Egyptians supposedly didn't know Pi. Someone came up with a pretty good explanation: Perhaps they used a wheel as a measuring tool, just as you see used today. One revolution = whatever the circumference of the wheel. When you measure using a circle, you get pi built in to your construction.

But there was enough in his voluminous evidence to impress me.   Much of what he had to say rang true.   It just seemed that the foundation was too slim for the edifice.   Then, suddenly the mode changed.

What follows is an effort on my part to convey the essence of our conversation. Mind you, I was struggling with a language barrier and having to rely on René & Yheni to translate.   Profi is far too dignified to speak in the crude vernacular I use here, but setting it down just so is an attempt to express the core of the experience.

Profi lays his mouse aside and turns foursquare to me with his bright eyes and his impressive humanity and says, "You think I'm going too far with this theory, don't you? I know how you feel. It seems like this vessel has long ago been filled, and any more is simply spilling onto the ground. I have an answer to the very question that you are too polite to ask," he says. "And I also know what your real question is." He wags his finger on "real question" and Profi is beginning to lose it with me.   He pries lose another nail from our bond.   "But first," he says. "Let me ask you....have you read the bible?"

Oh, Por Favorrrr, I think.   I come to learn about rocks and you want to wet-towel me with the Rock of Ages? I ruffle myself and allow as how, "One of my grandfathers was a Presbyterian minister.   The other was a deacon in the Methodist church.   I was president of the Sunday school when I was twelve.   My father, recovering from years of alcoholism, married a fat Christian Scientist, converted with a medieval zeal and did his best to drag me along with him."

"And I'll bet you didn't go along with him, did you?" says Profi.

Before I can give my answer he says, "But you learned something about Buddhism from your father's embrace of Christian Science, didn't you?"

"Yes, that's true," I say. "But I was so turned off by the puritanical trappings of Mary Baker Eddy's thinking that I didn't get anything out of it until later. Then, in the 70's I steeped myself in Eastern thought. I actually spent a good part of a year reading inspirational literature at breakfast. I worked so hard at removing myself from involvement that I was beginning to lose interest in what happened to me. But after a while I did get the connection between Christian Science and Buddhism."

This little man, this giant of a human being is silent for a moment, filling that moment with a maddeningly knowing grin. "You are a Quester, you are. I can see that."

Quester? Moi? You must be joking.

"Let me get on with my point, says Profi. You may want to take notes."

Once again, my pen is poised, my spiral notebook and myself are open to a blank page.

"This is a funny story," says Profi. "A long time ago...when we Homo-sapiens, we self-conscious, self-aware, self-important, opposing-thumbed, evolutionary-peak-of-the-moment critters were very young, we got together and had this meeting. At this meeting, which went on longer than a hundred faculty meetings, we decided that things here on earth weren't quite up to our liking.

There must be more to it than this. This is Hell. Big critters are eating little critters and bad guys seem to have some kind of advantage. We've got to do something about this."

Then he says, "Have you ever read Jean Jacques Rousseau?"

I am so thankful. Thank you, Profi, for hitting me with the right question. I get to raise my hand again. "Yes....some. I read *The Confessions,* and I read about the neo-romanticists that preceded the French Revolution." Profi was kind enough to let me parade my little knowledge and go on. "They believed that we were screwed up because we had left the natural state where we used to be living in perfect and loving harmony with lions and cobras and the Neanderthals in the next valley. It made me think of Genesis when that bitch Eve handed poor old innocent dorky Adam the apple from the tree of knowledge... I took a breath. The air is thin up here at 12,000 feet and I am unable to pontificate with my usual vigor and perseveration.

"And mankind fell," said Profi. "Right?"

"That's the way the story goes."

Profi leans forward until I can clearly see the hairs in his nose. He grins. His eyes dance. He says, "As you gringos would say, that is bullshit. *Caca de Vaca!*"

I recoil. For such profanity to erupt from this sweet, erudite, well-mannered septuagenarian is shocking. Is he running down an effect on me?

Profi rises from his stool, shifts his little camel's hair golf cap to a jauntier angle and almost bellows: "<u>*Caca de Vaca!* Man did not fall. Man didn't have enough sense to make a decision about eating knowledge. We are here because it was God's idea....and for us to think that we had anything to do with our condition by eating some lady's apple is pure Homo-hubris.</u>"

I liked that "Homo-hubris" part and was ruminating on it when Profi sits back down and reseats his cap to a more monastic slant. "So let me get back to my story," he says. "There were these newly evolved humans, and they were a little outraged at the trials they were forced to bear. They were so recently out of the womb....out of the cradle.....off the teat, so to speak, that they still harbored a few early memories of what it was like back then before they got to this sorry state of earthly toil and tribulation. And here's what they decided at the end of that meeting:

"There must be some way out of here.

"And because these Humans were stronger of arm than of brain here's what they came up with: They would simply build a tower so tall that it would be their stairway back up to the big guy in the sky. Then everything would be okay again."

Profi chuckles. "I can just imagine God up there, looking down on these fools, and letting them struggle with their harebrained project until they were so exhausted they would listen to good sense. And you know what he does next, don't you? He made them speak different languages so that they couldn't understand each other, and after that they couldn't cooperate and couldn't finish the tower. Now, the question is, why did God do that?

"He's saying to these babies: 'I didn't send you down here to try to figure out a way to get back to me. I SENT YOU DOWN HERE TO BE MY EYES! I want you to smell and touch and hear this earth I gave you. AND I ALSO SENT YOU DOWN HERE TO SEE WHAT YOU COULD DO BY WAY OF IMPROVING THE MIX

"I have given you a world that is imperfect. Little things like air currents eddying off a bird's wing can swell up and cause one hell of a lot of misery to the whole earth. The planetary system you live in has a custard pie up its sleeve and you just never know when that pie is going to smack you in the face. If Comet Schumacher-Levy didn't get that point across, then you're dumber than the Neanderthals. And mind you, they have been much under-rated. So if you don't get the point that this is an urgent matter and time's a-wasting, so much for you."

Profi cuts it off like the end of a Beatle mix. He is not soapboxing this message. He is calm and there is a teasing smile flickering over his face.

"Okay, Mr. Sunday School President," says Profi. "Do you know the parable of the talents?"

I do my best to will humility into my voice and say, "Of course. It's about using what strengths you've been God-given." And being a life-long penny-ante poker player, I flip out my dear little metaphor and add, "It's about playing the cards you've been dealt to the best of your ability."

Profi, without a ripple of disagreement leaps up and leaps in. "*Exactamente!* Use what God Given talents you have to improve yourself, your family, your friends, your fellow human beings......your Planet. And if you ever get that far we'll go on to bigger things."

I am getting all excited because it feels like we are in sync like a couple of cheerleaders. I'm swigging air and I don't know whether it's the altitude or the sense of impending epiphany.

Epiphany is sometimes comical. Actually, I think sometimes the best epiphanies present themselves in comedy because if you laugh, I mean if you totally surrender to laughter, your mind takes just enough of a vacation for the message...the epiphany, to get through to your heart. On the flip side, think about this: At one time there was a strong and authoritative belief that Christ did not laugh....never....not once. That time was the middle, or more accurately, the dark ages. There you go.

Profi has paused for me to take these notes. Then he goes on. He speaks so quietly that I have to ask for a repetition. He is speaking again for the Almighty.

"Don't think so much about me. If I wanted you to sit around and think about me all the time I would have given you a perfect world where food dropped off trees into your hands and you didn't have to think about tending your crops. But look around you, dummy. Do you see any food dropping into your hands? Do you see real love diplomas that are free? No you do not. I gave you a challenge and I don't want to hear any more of your whining and cringing and trying to ignore the basic fact of your existence. You were sent here on a mission and it isn't necessarily either easy or pleasant. And if it were too easy and pleasant you would all be bored and boring people.

"Don't be too occupied with getting answers to transcen-dental questions. Quit fawning over gurus. Get up off your knees and go out there and do something with your life! Being God, I know about the possibility of second chances, and my advice would be to consider that a non-reality."

Profi's fervor subsides. He retreats from his voice of God and turns to his obsolete computer. You can tell he has a fondness for this device. He sighs and opens a calendar program that displays the entire year. He points to it and looks at me with a Cheshire cat grin. "What happens at the end of this?"

I don't know what he's getting at.

"At the end of this year of nineteen hundred, ninety nine, Anno Domini," he says. "We drop off the face of reality, don't we. *Two thousand years, we're talking about here.* NOW what happens?"

My hand is halfway up but he goes on: "*Something* has got to happen. After all, how often do we come to the beginning of the second millennium?"

"But...." I say.

Profi jumps in. "But, but, but, of course. It's not the Chinese millennium, is it? It's not the Muslim millennium, is it? Who said when to start counting? That, however, is not going to stop the inundation of nonsense that attends our REALLY BIG calendar tallies.

"There are always two basic themes:

"*The world is going to end. (There you go Jupiter and your comet Schumacher-Levy)*

"*And...the first or second coming is at hand.*

"There may be truth in the first proposition, but I wouldn't count on the Gregorian calendar for the timing of an event of such magnitude as the end of the world.

"As for the second?   There is only one coming.   It has been coming for eons.   What is coming is the simple and obvious comprehension that we are all in this together.   The coming has been happening from the beginning.   Understanding is the coming.   Empathy is the coming.   Planetary community is the coming.   It has been going on since the Big Babel Schism.   There have been many contributions to the coming: runners, homing pigeons, smoke, semaphore and mirror signals,   papyrus scrolls,   monk scribes and their efforts to bind up the remaining thin threads of knowledge, moveable type, the pony express, telegraph, radio, television, the fax machine......All with one thing in common.   They have the power to connect us and hopefully, ultimately bring us together in common cause."

He clicks his way to his email. He reads something that amuses him.   For a moment he stares at, or through, his monitor.   Then he turns around, removes his glasses and rubs the bridge of his nose.

"And now we have this," he says.   "The internet is another coming. It brings familiarity and understanding. Maybe it will connect us all one day.   And that will be a very powerful unity."

He goes back to his computer to read some new bit of email. Then he turns to me again. "A message from a friend in Russia.   He tells me that I think too much about the stones."   He laughs. "But as you might say, the stones are my hand of cards, and I must play that hand well.   If some of what I write is useless, so be it.   But perhaps there will be a few worthy thoughts here and there, and maybe, God willing, there will be just one sparkling, heretofore unseen, jewel that will have made it all worthwhile and I can go to my grave knowing that I have done my best."

Profi looks at his watch and rises.   There is another student at the door and our time is up.   We exchange names and email addresses and he shakes my hand, then embraces me.

"May I come back to talk to you again?" I ask.

He grins and cocks his head to the side as if to deny me another audience.

We are being ushered out the door when he slaps me on the shoulder and says. "You may come back to talk, Señor Richard.....but only about the stones."

"Oh yes," I say, "About those stones...."

But I have lost him. This professor of physics is already ushering another adoring young female student into his *domaine*.

THE SECOND WEDDING

The Church at Tinta

I got back to Cusco in early September and hit the ground running to make the rounds of my favorite places, one of which is Rosie O'Grady's. When the proprietor, my friend Charlie Donovan, bustled in with his usual energy, he was all aglow. "Your timing is perfect." he said, "Next weekend Betty and I are getting married."

Charlie already has a wife and two young children, so I was surprised. "Aren't you already married?"

"We had a civil service in Ethiopia. Since Betty isn't Catholic, we couldn't have a church service there, and I wanted to... *we* wanted to have a religious service. It's going to be held in a very old church in Tinta."

I had never heard of Tinta.

"It's two hours from here by bus on the road to Puno. It's the birthplace of Tupac Amaru."

Tupac Amaru II, the great-great grandson of the last ruler, Inca Tupac Amaru, was the leader of a rebellion, sometime in the seventeenth century. When they finally defeated and captured the warrior, they brought him to Cusco. The story goes that they tied his limbs to four horses to quarter him. But Tupac Amaru was so strong that the horses had to struggle mightily to tear him apart. Supposedly his various body parts are buried in different places in Peru. Tinta is supposedly the repository of an arm... or maybe a leg.

"Why in Tinta?"

"We can't do it here in Cusco without a long process to confirm Betty into the church. However, it just so happens... we know a priest in Tinta who is somewhat irregular and will marry us without all the la de da."

"La de da," is one of Charlie's favorite phrases.

"He's Father Sean, and, being Irish, he naturally came into Rosie's one day. We became immediate friends. And also, another friend and priest from Lima are coming up to help with the service. That's Father Paul O'Leary."

"Father Paul will be coming up with Sister Sara. He's about sixty and she's... younger." Charlie's eyes were alight. "They're both lurvely people."

"Lurvely," in Irish means well mannered and interesting, I think.

"He is quite the character. You'll love him."

This turned out to be an understatement.

Shifting gears, Charlie asked the favor. "Would you be so kind as to take my old video camera and film the service?"

Charlie is one of my anchors in Cusco and I always welcome the chance to do him a good turn. "Of course. And I'll buy a couple of rolls of 35mm film and get stills as well." In fact, the thought of sitting through a long Catholic wedding, any long wedding for that matter, gives me the heebie-jeebies. As the official photographer, I would be able to keep moving around for good angles and could avoid all that kneeling, standing, sitting and bowing.

The night before the wedding Father Paul and Sister Sara appeared at Rosie's. He was slightly round, somewhat balding and altogether an imposing presence. Sister Sara was an attractive lady, maybe somewhere in her forties. She had a fine bosom, short hair and a perpetual gleam in her eye that seemed somewhat out of place for a bride of Christ. The Padre and I got into a deep conversation right off. I found that he was here in Peru working with the poor. He was a member of a group that was instigated by Bishop Fulton Sheen and funded by the Boston Diocese.

Respectfully, I asked, "What shall I call you?"

"Call me Paul. That's my name."

Right away, it was apparent that Paul had strayed from the strict line of the church. "I would ask people here in Peru, 'Are you good Christians?' And they would shake their heads and confirm their sinful ways. But then I would ask them, 'What would you do if a family of people from the hills came here to Lima and had no place to stay?' And they would admit that they would take them in until they found their own work and their own place. 'But what if you have your own family of five and only two rooms?' And they would say that they would somehow squeeze them in. Then I would say to them, 'This is the heart of Christianity.'" He waggled his finger. "This is giving on a level that I, and most people I know, would not rise to. You *are* good Christians and don't even know it."

Father Paul poured what remained of his beer into a glass. As he warmed to his subject, he leaned forward His words were spoken with intensity, his eyes directly on you. "I have been here in Peru for twenty-five years and I'll tell you, I have gleaned a whole new message from the bible, seeing it through the eyes of these people. It has changed my life and my faith." He downed the beer and ordered a brandy.

I was drawn to this man, drawn to him like a father, even though he was younger than myself. I suppose that's why they call them Padres. I asked, "Have you ever thought of writing a book about this experience? The world, especially the western world, seems to crave spiritual guidance."

"Well, the last one to do this, to write about our faith from the point of view of the Indians, was Father O'Day. And he was hounded out of the church."

"Would you care if that happened to you?"

A good swallow of his brandy. "I wouldn't give a rat's ass." His words exactly. This was no starched man of the cloth.

I put my hand on his shoulder as I stepped down from my bar stool to go to the bathroom. "Charlie told me I would like you." And he was so very, very right.

*   *   *   *

So on a bright Saturday morning at about 9:30, the big tourist bus left with a load of about 30 for Tinta. I sat next to, and struck up a friendship with Patricia, a pretty girl who runs a school in Cusco. I was in the very early stages of growing a beard and looked like some Aqualung just risen from the gutter, but this didn't seem to bother Patricia. We became quite com-fortable with each other.

The road to Tinta, at least the first part of it, was familiar to me. We passed the entrance to the Inca site of Tipon, a terraced and irrigated agricultural station set high above the valley. And we passed the crumbling adobe ruins of the pre-Inca town *Pikillacta*, which means "Flea Town." We followed the river Vilcanota, hardly more than a trickle in these early days of the rainy season, then past the little towns of *Oropesa* and *Pillipamba* that supply, respectively, bread and roof tiles to Cusco. The hills rose gently on both sides of the valley. Thanks to the first scattered rains, the greening had begun. We passed Lake Urcos on our right. Patricia pointed to it and told me that, according to legend, the gold chain of Huascar was beneath its waters. Huascar was the Inca whose brother Atlahualpa had warred with him for the throne and won... only to be captured and murdered by the Spanish. Considering the rapacious gold-lust of the Spanish, the smallness of Lake Urcos, and the alleged gargantuan size of Huascar's chain, I seriously doubt the story. But it might just be so. How many legends have turned out to be true? Maybe someday I'll come here with a one-man submarine and a metal detector and get rich.

The passengers were jolly, but it was a decidedly muted version of what was to be on the return trip. Father Paul and Sister Sara sat up front like a comfortable old married couple. The wedding cake sat to the driver's right on the engine cowling, carefully guarded by Faridé, the pretty waitress from Rosie's, who was riding shotgun. With video and still cameras dangling from my neck I staggered around the rocking bus taking pictures. Admittedly I took more of Patricia than necessary. It gave me the excuse to say to her, "*Tu es muy linda.*" And it's true, she is quite pretty. I am having a familiar recurrence of my long-standing delusion. I think I am still thirty-five.

On first sight Tinta is hardly impressive. We turned off the road to the right, crossed the railroad tracks and drove down a narrow street lined with two-story, painted adobe shops and dwellings. In a few blocks we came to the Plaza de Armas. It was huge, maybe the size of a couple of football fields side by side. It was paved, but otherwise nearly devoid of adornment or variation. And it was practically unpopulated. In all this vastness, there were fewer than ten people scattered about.

Three sides of the square were lined with two-story adobe buildings. On the fourth was the church and the rectory. Fronting the church, rising from a high pedestal, were three crosses, a noteworthy feature of this little town. An engraving of this looming reminder of crucifixion once adorned a bill of a now-defunct Peruvian currency.

As we got off the bus, we were greeted by a slim man wearing a plaid shirt, a battered felt hat, and glasses that dwarfed his narrow face. He placed his hand on my shoulder, in what I thought was the prelude to a hug, but was, I think, a form of priestly greeting. This was Father Sean, priest of this parish, and, as I was to discover, a first class human being. He was, indeed, "a lurvely pearson".

We were led to Father Sean's room where I could stash some of my equipment and the wedding participants could change clothes. I noticed a TV, a VCR, a shelf of religious books and a popular mystery novel.

I went about capturing candid photos and video footage of the site and the wedding participants and guests. In time the big side doors to the church were opened and I went in to survey the location. It was dark. Very dark. Thankfully, I had brought rolls of very fast film, but I had my doubts about the possibilities of video footage. My eyes gradually adjusted to the light and I could see that this was an impressive church indeed. The walls were lined with huge oil paintings of religious scenes, framed with massive gilt frames, many of them, I was told, dating from the sixteen hundreds. The nave was all gilt and stained glass through which, sadly for the photographer, no light shone. Father Sean came along, still in his plaid shirt but hatless, and informed me as he pointed toward the distant ceiling, that there would be more light for the ceremony. I looked up and noticed for the first time the rows of circular fluorescent lights hanging from long cords from the ceiling. *Fluorescent Lights!* Bane of photographers. Much as I was reluctant to do so, I would have to use the flash on my still camera and simply pray that some-thing could be seen in the video footage.

Father Paul came into the church and looked around with admiration. "My God! Look at this. What a church! Rich people would pay a million dollars to be married here." I suspected Charlie was getting it for somewhat less.

There was still some time before the ceremony, so I went back outside for more video footage. Suddenly the viewfinder showed the symbol of a battery with a slash through it. I had fully charged the damn thing the night before, but it was an old battery. I dashed back to Father Sean's room and retrieved the charger. Back in the church, I asked Father Sean how long before the service would begin. Fifteen minutes, I was told. I plugged the charger into an extension cord that snaked along the nave and powered the PA system. More power was called for if I was to get all the service recorded.

Fathers Sean and Paul disappeared into the rectory and re-emerged in several minutes in splendid gold-trimmed white robes. These two ordinary looking men were transformed, shining, with their ecclesiastical authority now manifest. Father Sean alerted me. "Five minutes to service."

I waited two minutes and snatched the battery from the charger. It was far from completely charged, but it would have to do. I jammed it into the camera and crossed my fingers. (Crossed fingers is a sort of protestant version of making the sign of the cross.)

The service commenced, and oh, I was so thankful to be a photographer and not a participant. (I have an unfortunate dislike of ceremony. It's a character flaw, I suppose.) I was parsimonious with my video recording, grabbing a few seconds here and there and relying more on stills shots with flash. I captured most of Charlie's vows and the cursed "battery low" symbol appeared. I kept shooting as Betty began her vows. And as if ordained by the Almighty, Betty and the Battery finished together.

The wedding over, the revelry of the reception began. Outside, a long table was set up beneath a canvas awning that was being whipped furiously by wind. The tablecloth had to be pinned down with weights.

I was standing next to Charlie. "We came out here yesterday to set things up," He said. "There was no wind and you could fry an egg on the pavement."

Nevertheless, Piña Colada's were served and the jollity commenced. The two padres had shorn their robes and, once again, seemed just like regular folks. I joined them and chanced telling an old joke:

A Catholic girl took her Protestant boy friend to a mass. The church was horribly hot and with all the kneeling, standing, and sitting, the boy began to sweat profusely. But he was doing his best to follow the service and to please his girlfriend. After a while, sweat began to trickle into his eyes. He took out a handkerchief, mopped his brow and then dropped it in his lap. His girlfriend glanced down, and seeing the white against his dark trousers, whispered to him: "Is your fly open?"

"No," replied the boy. "Is it supposed to be?"

They laughed... genuinely, I think.

What with all the wind, it seemed obvious that the wedding dinner would have to be moved inside. The guests began carrying chairs, tables and tableware. The Padre pitched in. Along came Father Paul toting a stack of plates. Gary, one of the groomsmen, carried an even larger stack, and Sister Sara carried a Piña Colada. I only wished that the Padre had been wearing his robe to complete the incongruity.

The dinner was fabulous...chicken, trout, salad and the obligatory potatoes. Wine, beer, and pisco sours flowed into each and every gullet. Patricia moved from her place to one next to me. I am thankful for the attention this pretty young girl is giving me. Speeches were made and from what was said, Charlie and Betty sounded like two of the finest people God had ever created. And in truth, I would have to agree. This wonderful family was expecting to return to Ireland soon, and I, along with much of Cusco, would feel the loss. Rosie's would never be the same.

The plan was for us to take the train back. This seemed strange in that the train took an hour longer than the bus, and in that the bus was leaving immediately with mostly empty seats. I was soon to see why we were taking the train.

We walked down to the tracks and waited. I asked Charlie if he would consider lying down on the tracks for a picture. And unbelievably, Charlie, still in his wedding suit, spread-eagled himself on the tracks. "That's marriage in a nutshell," someone said.

Finally there is a whistle and we see the train approaching. This, I was told, was the first time the train had ever stopped in Tinta.

We were guided to a certain car and one and all gasped upon entering. This was no ordinary train car, this was a re-creation of an Orient Express car. (I later discovered that the British company Orient Express, was a part-owner of Peru Rail) It was all nineteenth century ambiance: mahogany paneling, brass luggage racks, upholstered armchairs, a brocade ceiling and tables with linen and crystal. Patricia motioned me to a seat at her table. Father Paul, sitting behind me with Sister Sara there at his side, kept saying, "I would *never, never* have thought...." All this had been arranged by Yasmine, an executive with Peru Rail, and a good friend of Charlie and Betty's. It seems that Charlie and Betty have a lot of good friends.

The drinks and the food kept coming, and the revelry went over the top. A group of airline executives were clustered ahead of me in the car, knocking back the booze with great gusto. Occasionally, for no reason I could tell, they would rise out of their seats in unison, throw up their arms and let out a great shout. It was The Mexican Cheer, they said.

Charlie sang a sweet Irish song, mostly in key.   Father Paul sang an Irish drinking song.

After three or four more pisco sours, I needed bathroom relief. I went to the rear of the car but found the mahogany door of the bathroom locked.   I could hear laughter within from several voices. A few minutes later the door opened and two men and a woman emerged in a cloud of marijuana smoke.   I went in, did my necessaries and got high on the air.

Three hours later, we pulled into the Cusco train station and Charlie's wedding was officially over.   But the revelry went on till dawn.   This was, after all, an Irish wedding.

*   *   *   *

Some months later, when I was in the US, Charlie and Betty got married <u>again</u>.   It was a civil wedding in Cusco... something to do with getting Peruvian residency for Betty.

*I can imagine the **fourth** wedding, with the two of them standing on a seaside cliff in County Cork, Ireland...Charlie's true home. Thunder and lightening, God's kettledrums and fireworks, rattle and flash about the matrimonial site.   The beaming couple wear Celtic robes that are whipped by the wind.   In the familiar cadences of the ancient language, the classic matrimonial admonitions and encouragements flow from the mouth of the hoary priest.*

And they respond gravely and appropriately, even as they are both thinking....

...Of their fifth wedding.

ATLANTIS

Charlie and I were sitting at a table talking about Inca walls.

"I'm sick of Inca rocks," says Charlie.

I suspect he's just sick of hearing me talk about them.

"Are you crazy, Charlie? Without those rocks you wouldn't be having a bar in this town.

He was about to snort a reply when a tall man approach-ed us and addressed Charlie.   "Excuse me, you are the owner of this place, aren't you?"

Charlie, ever the gentleman, and perhaps glad to get a break from Inca rocks, stood up and extended his hand. "Charlie Donovan," he said. "I'm owner and manager."

"My name is John Froelich. May I join you?" He had a well-used, old briefcase with him, a sight oddly incongruous in a bar in Cusco, Peru.   It seemed more suited to an ivy-league classroom.

"Of course," Charlie offered a chair and introduced me.

John Froelich had a wide mouth, jam full of teeth, readily shown. His hair was short and brown and he had an odd way of turning to look at you, moving his shoulders with his head as though his neck was too stiff to move his head independently.   Above his eyes flourished a bountiful, black crop of eyebrows.   On one side a lock of eyebrow dipped toward his eye so that on first glance he appeared to have been punched.   He had an open and friendly air befitting a salesman or politician. I guessed him to be in his early fifties.

"I always make it a policy to get to know the owner of the bar... *if* he's likeable, and the word abroad is that you are just that."

Charlie, not unsusceptible to kind words, called over the pretty young waitress Lili and ordered a round on the house.   John and I thanked Charlie as we watched the girl's retreat. Lili has one of the finest sterns in Cusco. John's massive eyebrows elevated slightly in appreciation.   Then he turned to Charlie. "You're from Ireland?"

"Cork." Charlie was sitting back, legs and arms folded.

John leaned forward. "Delicious place. I visited for the first time two years ago. You must miss it."

"Sometimes. Where are you from?"

"The states. One is almost afraid to admit it abroad."

"Stand tall, John." I gave him a quick, fraternal dip of the head. "What brings you here?"

John Froelich took a deep breath and smiled in a way that said he had heard and answered this question many times. He leaned back, arms folded, head tucked into his chin. "I'm an archaeologist. A former university professor, now defrocked."

Lili appeared with our drinks. John tilted his head toward her and produced that large set of teeth. "Thank you, Dear."

When she was gone Charlie, the Catholic, asked, "Defrocked?"

"Well, of course, not defrocked. That's the wrong word if you want to take it literally. I was more or less hounded out of the profession."
He was smiling as if proud of this state of affairs. I could smell an interesting evening in the air. "That's pretty strong stuff," I said. "Weren't you tenured."

"I was, so my position was more or less secure. But when your peers, to a man, regard you with open hatred and gnashing teeth, the security isn't worth it. I quit." His volume was up a notch and I noticed that he had gotten the attention of a group at the next table. They had suddenly hushed. You could see John's professor-self emerging. His voice went up another notch. He leaned forward and touched my arm in a gesture meant to ingratiate and command attention. "Archeologists are worse than fundamentalist believers. You know how it goes. Dr. Philpot digs into the earth a few meters and makes a discovery that leads him to a theory, that leads to a paper, that leads to a book, that leads to a career. A few years later, another digger goes down a few more meters in the same area and comes up with evidence that refutes Dr. Philpot's lifetime work. He is promptly accused by the good Doctor of shoddy science. But it doesn't usually stop there. The man is also accused of being a liar, a moron and perhaps even a thief and plunderer. If you want to see a really nasty war, attend an archaeologist's convention. The vituperation, open and backhanded, is very, very ugly. I know. I have been a frequent recipient."

This was a man after my own heart. I was beginning to like John Froelich. I said, "It's like … what's his name? The man who proposed the continental drift theory."

"Alfred Wegener. Another German and a courageous one. He was pilloried, of course, but gradually the laggards began to accept his ideas and the continental drift theory led to the science of plate tectonics."

"It seems like a pretty obvious thing," said Charlie, "If you just look at a map."

The next table had by now dropped into total silence, giving John their full attention.

"Exactly!" John almost shouted. He had been given a cue and was further warming to his passion, which was yet to be revealed. For a moment, no one spoke.

I finally asked the beggared question. "So what was it you did to offend the academic community?"

He paused for effect before answering my question, giving himself a bit of a dramatic boost. Suddenly we were interrupted by the appearance of my old friend Miguel, none other than Popcorn Boy. He was standing there mute, with the proffered bag and the irresistible eyes. One of the waiters came to remove him, but John intervened. "Wait! I love popcorn." He bought two bags. I grinned at Miguel as he was ushered out.

"Now back to your offence," I said.

John straightened up and angled his glance toward me. "I used the 'A' word."

"The 'A' word?" said Charlie?

"Atlantis." He let the 'A' word hang in the air like a condor in a thermal.

One of the people at the next table slid his chair over. "Mind if I get in on this?"

He was a young man in his twenties with an encouraging eagerness about him. He wore John Lennon glasses and had his long blond hair tied in a ponytail.

John was obviously glad to be back at the lectern. "I certainly don't. Why don't you join us."

"Please," said Charlie. He summoned one of the waiters to help and we joined two tables so that the six of us now sat as though at a seminar. John took the head position. He lifted his briefcase and placed it before him, promising revelations from within its folds.

Charlie leaned back in his chair and crossed his arms, in a

'show me' pose. I leaned forward, elbows on the table. The idea of Atlantis has always interested me.

Ponytail was wide-eyed with anticipation.

"I wrote a paper entitled 'Indications of an Atlantean outpost in the Pacific'."

"In the Pacific?" Ponytail's voice went up on the last word.

"Exactly. And that is a clue as to why I am in Cusco." He took a sip of his drink, set it down and withdrew an unopened pack of American Spirit cigarettes. "Do you mind if I smoke?"

We all shrugged an assent and John Froelich took his time tapping the pack on the tabletop, carefully pulling the cellophane tab and tearing off the top. He gave one side a sharp smack that lifted several cigarettes in a perfect stepped pattern. "Would you like one? They have no chemicals like saltpeter in them. You put a burning American Spirit in an ashtray and it goes out. And you don't ruin your sex life."

"Unfortunately, I have none to ruin at the moment," I said. "But I quit smoking fifteen years ago after a three-pack-a-day habit."

"I'd like to hear about that," said John. "I'm trying to quit." He was testing our interest.

"Another time. Tell us about Atlantis in the Pacific."

"Outpost," he corrected. "Atlantis should be considered a catchall word. There was probably more than one 'prehistoric' civilization. As you no doubt know, popular writers have placed Atlantis just about everywhere on earth. A tiny thread of evidence is uncovered and that thread, supported by any detail, no matter how tenuous or spurious, is supposedly proof of the hypothesis. The latest is a book proclaiming Atlantis to have been in the middle of Lake Titicaca."

"I read the book," said Ponytail. "It was by an English air force cartographer, wasn't it"

John took a thoughtful drag on his cigarette. "It was inretesting. He found parallels to Plato's description. It was a bit of a stretch though, to make it Plato's Atlantis. But he did find evidence of an ancient civilization. Another indication, I think of the pervasiveness of earlier civilizations."

Ponytail was caught up in it. "Okay, so there was more than one. But was there a center?"

John stood up with a knowing smile on his face. He took a drag of his cigarette, placed it in the ashtray to self-extinguish, and reached into his briefcase. Taking his time for dramatic effect, he rummaged until he came up with a rolled up paper, which he laid out on the table, battening down the corners with ashtrays.

"This," he said, "Is the Piri Reis map.

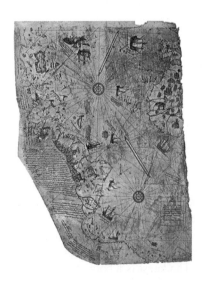

"The Piri Rais map was discovered in a Turkish monastery in 1929. It was drawn by a Turkish admiral of that name, who said it was copied from older maps. Note well, that *it was copied from older maps*.

Now along comes this fellow named Charles Hapgood, who taught science history at Keane state teacher's college in New York State. Hapgood made the map a student project that went on for a decade, more or less.

"The map was sent to military cartographers for expert opinion. The answer that came back was shocking, and it was made without comment from these experts." Another pause for effect. Another sip of drink and drag of cigarette.

John stared off into space for a few moments to let our curiosity build. "The cartographers stated simply that whoever had drawn the original maps had an understanding of our planet that wasn't equaled until recent times. They had a fix on longitude, which, as you know, bedeviled sailors until sometime in the middle of the eighteenth century. But that's only part of it. The map showed islands in the Atlantic that are no longer there. It showed rivers flowing into the ocean without today's deltas... deltas that have taken thousands of years to accumulate. It showed the continental shelf of South America as being *above water*. And get this... It showed the landmass of that part of Antarctica nearest the southern tip of South America. Not the glacial mass. The actual *landmass*. The landmass beneath the glaciers of Antarctica was only charted by modern man in the 1950's.

"The Piri Rais map shows our planet with a lower sea level, and an Antarctica that was partially temperate. The reason it was partially temperate, Hapgood believed, is because the poles of the earth were in a different location. The North Pole was in the Hudson Bay. Siberia was temperate. That's why frozen mammoths were found with food in their mouths and bellies that could not possibly have grown in the Siberian climate that exists today. The crust of the earth had shifted, most likely very suddenly. Hapgood's theory gained the respect of Albert Einstein, who wrote a preface to one of his books. Hapgood thought the shift was caused by internal forces deep in the earth. Personally, I think it was from extra-terrestrial forces."

Ponytail jumped in. "Like a comet or meteorite." .

"Perhaps. Or maybe even a fragment of a supernova that entered our solar system. We can still see the remnants of such a supernova in the constellation Vela. It's a pretty good candidate. Whatever the cause, something dramatic occurred to the earth around

9600 BC. It ended the ice age and eradicated vast species of flora and fauna. The Mastodon, the Wholly Mammoth, the Saber Toothed Tiger, and the Giant Tree Sloth, among others disappeared. This event also had profound effects on the earth's crust. That, gentlemen, is what brings me to Cusco."

"Okay," said Charlie. I'll bite. How is it that changes in the Earth's crust bring you to Cusco."

"You yourself said that Wegener's continental drift theory seemed obvious if you looked at a map. Western Europe and Africa fit neatly into the North and South American contin-ents. My theory is based on just such an obvious feature of the globe. Only in this case, the feature is now beneath the surface of the ocean." He withdrew from his briefcase another map, moved his drink and cigarettes aside and laid the map face-down on the table. John Froelich was a master of suspense. "But before I show you this map, let me ask you a question. You, Charlie, have lived here for a while, I gather, so you must be well-acquainted with the stone constructions in these parts."

Charlie gave a reluctant nod.

"Do you know of anywhere else in the world where such stoneworks exist? I mean walls of stone that look just like these old Inca walls in Cusco?"

Charlie shook his head.

"There is only one other place. Can you guess where that is? If you don't know, you'd probably never guess." Yet another sip of his drink, another ritualistic lighting of his cigarette.

"I give up," said Charlie. "You tell us."

John put down his drink. "It is the most remote inhabited place on earth. Its occupants referred to it as 'The Navel of the World'. Does that sound familiar?

"It's what the Incas called Cusco," said ponytail.

"Exactly! This place also had the totora reed and the potato when the first western sailors discovered it in the seventeen-hundreds."

"Rapa Nui!" shouted Ponytail. "Isla de Pescua! Easter Island!"

"You get an A plus," said John. "Just 'Easter Island' would have gotten you an 'A'."

"The people who carved all those statues...."

"The Moai," said John. But those who carved the statues probably did not build the one or two extant walls of the Andean type." He turned the map over.

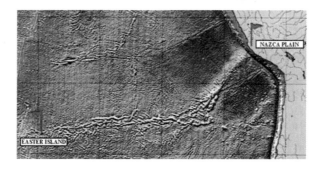

This is part of a map made by the NOAA. That's the National Oceanographic and Atmospheric Administration of the United States. It is a map of that part of our earth invisible to us because it is underwater. Take a look here. This is lake Titicaca, and over here is the coast of Peru. The red flag marks the location of the Nazca Plain with all its strange lines and drawings. The other flag marks Easter Island... over two thousand miles from the western coast of Peru out in the Pacific. And what do you see between those two red flags?"

We sat contemplating this for a few moments.

Ponytail broke the silence. "How far below the ocean are those yellow lines?"

"Approximately two hundred to two thousand feet. What does this suggest to you?"

"A land bridge, maybe. But how did it get below the surface?"

John sat down without answering the question. "May I order another drink before we go on?" He summoned Lili, and in a very unusual gesture for a professor, bought a round for the table. "We'll just take a little class break until the drinks come."

I would have none of that. "Come on, John. Out with it."

Thus appropriately begged, he rose and continued. "We need another map to help explain the answer." He replaced the NOAA map and drew from his briefcase another. "Back to tectonics," he said. "You see here in the center is the Nazca Plate. It's subducting... diving under... the South America Plate. It's the most rapidly moving of all the earth's tectonic plates. The Nazca Ridge runs right through the middle of it and Easter Island sits on the western edge.

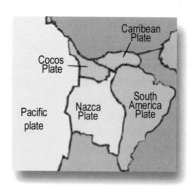

"Now think about this. Go back to our earlier discussion of worldwide catastrophe... the ending of the last ice age, the rise in sea level. The combination of a good shake and elevated oceans would be ideal circumstances to lower and inundate what might once have been... *most likely was*... a land bridge.

"And think about this. Here you have at one end and the other of that ridge, striking examples of unexplained and obsessive behavior. The Nazca Plain with all its lines and drawings, and Easter Island with its myriad, identical stone statues.

"And finally, tantalizingly, the stone walls like no other in the world.

"Gentlemen, the conclusion is staggering, but to me it is inescapable: Those walls, at least some of them, were built by a civilization that existed over twelve thousand years ago. Put that in your pipe and smoke it."

We figuratively, one or two of us literally, scratched our heads. "You wrote a paper on this?" I asked.

"Not only wrote a paper, but addressed a convention of archaeologists. It effectively ended my teaching career." He bowed, stowed his maps and sat down.

We all applauded him.

Once again Charlie folded his arms and settled back in his chair. "We still don't know exactly why you're here in Cusco, now, do we?"

John grinned at him. "I'll get to that. In a roundabout way. Are you aware of the discovery just made off the western coast of Cuba?" He addressed the question to the table at large and we all shook our heads. (This was mid-December 2001.) "A Canadian company called Advanced Digital Communications has been working with the Cuban government to find shipwrecks from the Colonial era.

The object, of course, is gold. But they've found something they hadn't counted on. They found the real thing. A sunken city. Pyramids, columns, vast open spaces and walls of huge cut stone." He sat back with a satisfied look. "I consider it a validation of my ideas. Whatever caused that city to subside was probably what caused the subsidence of the Nazca ridge. Just think about it... the tremendous, built-up tension of the Nazca plate pushing under the South American plate." He brought his fist down on the table, rattling glasses and startling us all. "Something strikes the earth with great force and suddenly the Nazca plate lurches down and under.

"Gentlemen, I am in Cusco for money. Money for underwater exploration off the eastern coast of Easter Island. If there was a connection between Peru and Easter Island, there's a good chance of finding gold. I'm presenting a slide show at the Monasterio Hotel this Sunday afternoon. The place will be full of rich Japanese tourists." He reached into his shirt pocket and pulled out a stack of invitations. You're all welcome to attend. Even if you have no intention of investing." He passed around the cards.

You are invited to a presentation by
John Froelich, PhD
on the connection between
CUSCO and ATLANTIS
Monasterio hotel.
Sunday, August 19th at 3:00 P.M.

TRUCKING TO LA PAZ WITH MAD MAX

For the last three years I've been making one feeble attempt after another to see the ruins of Tiawanaku. I had visit-ed La Paz in the early 80's, and had spent several days there with friends I had met in the U.S. I had crossed Titicaca in the hydro-foil, seen the Island of the Sun, the Island of the Moon and Copacabana. But I had yet to see Tiawanaku. It was a big hole in my education. I had read about the site, had even spent $300 for Arturo Posnansky's book "Tiawanaku, Cradle of American Man," had seen many photographs, but still lacked that first-hand experience.

I kept trying to locate my old friends in Bolivia, but they were not to be found. I had planned to go in January when Jim would be in Cusco and could join me. But then I got an offer I couldn't refuse.

My Aussie friend Glenn offered me a ride in his tourist truck. This is a monster Mercedes, a vehicle capable of carrying over twenty tourists with their gear. It is the size of, looks like, and actually is, a cargo container with windows. I had once ridden from Cusco to Ollantaytambo in the back of one of these ungainly things. It was piloted by Glenn. It's a two and a half hour trip by bus, but only an hour and a half at Glenn's hands. At the outset of that trip I was unsettled by his speed. But I soon realized that the man knew his business. He had driven big trucks all over Australia, and he was a true professional. He drove that behemoth like a racecar, flattening the curves, breaking coming in and accelerating through and out. I've never before seen anyone drive a truck like that.

Glenn drove one of two trucks that are owned by a South American touring company. One of the two had burnt out a bearing in the transmission and was awaiting repairs in Cusco. The other driver had packed all the tourists into the functioning truck and taken off for La Paz. The necessary parts had been requisitioned from Lima. The truck would be repaired in Cusco and Glenn would drive it to La Paz to rejoin the group and drive on south to Chile, then to Rio for carnival, the climax of a three-month trip.

If all went according to plan, the truck would be ready to leave Monday afternoon. We would leave with an hour or so of daylight remaining. We should make Puno, Peru by nine in the evening. We'd spend the night there, get up early and make La Paz at least by noon the next day. If all went according to plan...

Monday afternoon we got the word that the part hadn't been shipped. The trip was delayed a day, but there was still time to make it. He had to make La Paz by noon Wednesday. He explained to me that they had already broken down the transmission and it would only take a couple of hours to get it back together once the part arrived.

Tuesday afternoon I ran into Glenn having a burger at Norton Rat's Tavern. He said the tranny part was on the plane from Lima and we should be on our way by 4:30 that afternoon. He asked me to meet him at the garage at 4:15. The *Volvo Autriso* Garage. Near the Statue of the Condor on Avenida de la Cultura. No problem for me. I had been packed and ready for a whole day and had only unpacked my toothbrush.

I got a cab at four. I was carrying my backpack, two cameras and a plastic box with leftovers from lunch. "Volvo Garage," I told the driver. *"Cerca el Condor."*

We stopped beneath the tall cement column with the bronze condor statue atop. There, directly beneath it, was a narrow garage marked "Volvo." The steel door was pulled down and locked. It is impossible to miss that monster truck of Glenn's and it was not in sight.

"This has to be it," I said. I paid the driver and got out. I walked over and looked at the garage. It was definitely locked. I asked a couple of bystanders if there was another entrance. There wasn't.

The taxista yells to me. He's been holding in place, hoping for more fare when I give up on this garage. He's gotten out of his cab and noticed that I've left my box of leftovers on the roof. He walks over with it. Chips, Salsa and a cold taco.

We ask the men standing there if there isn't another Volvo garage nearby. They shake their heads. I'm mulling over Glenn's instructions. *"Volvo Autriso,"* I mumble.

"Oh!" says the driver. *"Volvo Autriso!"* He points up the street in the direction we've come from. *"Allá!*

It's about a half a mile back toward town. I don't know how we had missed it coming. The driver reminds me that I had told him it was near the condor. Near is relative.

Volvo Autriso is a big dealership/garage with a gate, a guard, and a few new cars up front and six or seven trucks undergoing surgery in the big covered garage at the back. The driver takes me to where the trucks are and I spot Glenn's truck. The red cab is tilted forward and several mechanics are poking around beneath. I get out and give the driver another two Sols. He was smart to wait. Or maybe he was smart enough to figure the whole thing out from the start.

Glenn is not in sight. I go into the waiting room and ask for him. I get laughs and shrugs. When I go back out, a taxi pulls up and Glenn disembarks with several big plastic containers of transmission fluid.

"They broke the line, those dumbfucks. It's gonna be a while." Glenn is covered with grease. There's a break in the seam of the seat of his pants and his bare butt is showing through. "These assholes don't know how to do anything. I'm having to show them how to put the tranny back together." He lifts what must be a hundred pounds of fluid and strides toward his truck.

It was four thirty by now. I followed Glenn and asked for a prognosis.

"Forty five minutes. Maybe an hour. Just take it easy mate. We can still make Puno by ten, ten thirty." He dives into the bowels of the engine and I go off to read a book.

An hour and a half later I had finished one book and started another. I kept going back for an update and the time kept being pushed back. At one point Glenn said, "I figure we'll skip Puno and just keep going till we hit the border at Desaguadero. We can spend a few hours sleeping in the back of the truck. They don't open the border till six and I've got to be in La Paz by noon."

The shop is deserted now, except for Glenn and his three mechanics. Work lights below and within send shafts of light into the dark, giving the scene an eerie feel. It is raining. I remember how fast Glenn drives, and how it's late and I wonder how the truck handles curves on wet pavement. This trip is beginning to have all the earmarks of an adventure. I have mixed feelings. I like an adventure, but I don't like the thought of being maimed or killed in a truck mishap. Since I am able to write this, I obviously escaped death, but there was adventure of another, completely unexpected sort, ahead of us.

Another hour and I'm hungry enough to nibble at the cold taco. I'm sitting in the deserted reception room and I hear Glenn shouting, "FUCK!" The three know-nothing mechanics who are working with him pick up the epithet.

"Fuck. Fuck. Fuck," the mechanics are shouting. In their mouths, the word somehow lacks Glenn's conviction.

But I am drawn back to the scene of the action. There are bodies protruding from beneath and within the monster. There are grunts and shouts and the clang of tools against metal. The big red cab is still tilted up at a 45-degree angle. Glenn stands with a warm beer in hand raging over the ignorance of the mechanics.

I'm no help. When it comes to automotive machinery I am worse than these targets of Glenn's wrath. The only attempt I ever made was to adjust the valves on my VW pop top camper with my daughter reading instructions to me from "The Com-plete Idiot's Guide to Volkswagen Repair." Twenty-five miles later the engine blew. I figure the best I can do is keep out of the way, so I go back to my new book and try to get into it.

Some time later I am startled by the sound of the truck roaring by the reception room door. I grab my things and run out, thinking we are finally leaving. But no, it's only a test. Glenn slams on the brakes, throws it into reverse and screams backwards. He stops. "No good!" he shouts. "The fuckin lines need more bleedin!"

He leaves the fuckin bleedin to the useless mechanics and begins to clean himself. "Ere's what I figger," he says. "We'll take a taxi into town and have a good feed before we take off and then we'll drive all night. No urry, just take it easy so's we get to Desaguadero by dawn."

I like the taking it easy part, but I wonder about driving all night.

"Don't worry. Times I've driven three days with no sleep...an no drugs either."

Glenn is standing there lathering up with goop and washing off several layers of grease and he seems perfectly comfortable wearing only his T-shirt and ripped pants while I am freezing, even with my jacket on. The man is made of strong stuff.

After more rounds of bleeding the transmission lines and testing the truck, Glenn pronounces it ready. I timidly ask about the brakes, which he assures me are okay.

So we take a cab to town for a feed.

Glenn has changed clothes and gotten most of the grease off himself. "Ow's my face?" he says.

"Okay. You look like you need a shave."

Glenn wants to eat at Ukukus restaurant. Ukukus is up at the far end of a pedestrian street called Procuradores, nicknamed Gringo Alley. It begins at the west end of the Plaza de Armas and runs for a good city block. There must be about twenty restaurants along the way and every one of them has someone in the alley trying to guide, or lure, or beg or drag you into their restaurant. It's another Cusco gauntlet. Even before you enter Procuradores they attack, Keros, El Cuate, La Dolce Vita, Tratamundos.... And there's Wilfredo, hawking for his restaurant. I greet him with a hug. He tries to get us into his place, but Glenn's determined. "Naaa. We're goin to Ukukus."

*　　*　　*　　*

Glenn... I can't even tell you his last name. He looks sort of like Mel Gibson and he has not a little of that Mad Max attitude. Dive in. Go for it full bore. He's big with long blond hair and a long stride. His jaw is big, his mouth is big, and his teeth are huge. I can't understand half of what Glenn says. His vowels are flat and his sentences are full of Australian slang that might as well be Chinese as far as I'm concerned. I have to ask him to repeat and then to translate. He tells me I'm not the only one who has trouble understanding him. I suggested to him once that maybe it was an attention-getting device, like people I know who speak so softly that you have to lean toward them and listen intently. Glenn didn't respond. I asked him if he could understand me and he said yes, he could.

I hadn't know him for long at the time of this story. We had met in Norton's a few times half a year ago and then recently he came back into town. That was when I rode with him to Ollantaytambo and got my first taste of his driving. It was later that night in Ollantaytambo that I got my first real taste of his humanity.

We were in a bar owned by my friends Lance and Ricardo. *La Puzanga* promotes these drinks made from jungle plants. Lance warned me not to mix my usual vodka with the jungle brews. I should have listened to him. The mix didn't sit right with me and I, who consider myself an accomplished drinker, got knee-walking drunk.

Around two in the morning I realized that it was time for me to throw in the towel. I lurched off my stool and announced my intention to go back to my hostal, a walk of about ten minutes through the town and down a dark and deserted dirt road. Glenn took it upon himself to walk me home. There were others in this drinking bout that had known me longer who made no such offer. Maybe it was just that they respected my abilities. Or maybe it was that the big Aussie, the truck driver, the Mad Max amongst us, saw someone in need. He insisted upon walking me all the way to my door. Then he went back and slammed on with the group until five the next afternoon. I woke up the next morning, oddly enough without a hangover, but with a clear memory of how this guy stood up for me, practically walked for me. Later I got an inkling of why.

During the next week I continued seeing Glenn almost every day. One Saturday night around 10:30 he casually says, "I was supposed to go to *Porto Velho* tonight. One of the dancers is a friend. But I don't know...."

Porto Velho! A new disco out near the airport with a naughty reputation. I had in mind a strip joint, a lap-dancing club, maybe even a little bit of a whorehouse.

"Come on, Glenn. I'll go with you. I want to see this place."

That was all the push Glenn needed. We were on our way.

Porto Vehlo is one of the few clubs in town that charges to get in. Most of them claim that they do, but they have hawkers out on the street giving out free passes. But *Porto Velho* really charges. We paid our ten sols and entered. There was a large open room, a big dance floor flanked by wooden tables and white resin chairs. Soda and beer bottles on the tables and in the hands. A full, but not crowded, dance floor. Latin music. Samba. At the far end a bar, and high above the bar, a stage platform supporting seven beautiful, leggy girls... the dancers, all wearing the same yellow costumes, garments that revealed less skin than a bikini.

We worked our way to the bar and ordered beers. Then Glenn planted himself, his eyes locked onto one of the dancers, a wry smile on his big face.

We were the only two gringos in the place. The crowd around the bar wanted to clink glasses and shout "Salud!" Someone offered to stash my mochilla, my little backpack, so that I could dance with more freedom. Glenn tells me it's okay. The guy is a bouncer here, as well as a genuine cop. It seems that everyone wants to talk to us. It's all very friendly. I think of what it would probably be like in the states for two white boys to walk into a black club, or a Mexican club. Not like this... not in my experience.

A plump girl in overalls is dancing ferociously. A boy next to me points to her and says to me, "My seester. You want to dance with her."

You want my seester, meester? Maybe there's some truth to *Porto Vhelo's* whorehouse reputation

Then there she is, in front of me, and we are in a wild dance. Most girls here dance sort of near you, not with you. But not this one. She is looking directly into my eyes and locking onto my moves, dancing and laughing with abandon. We carry on to the end of the song and then she is off dancing with someone else. No *puta*, no whore here, I think. Then a little later, her brother, if that is what he is, asks me to buy him a beer. So that's the deal. The guy's selling dances with his sister for beers. It seems harmless enough, so I buy the beer. It was worth it. The little chubette was great to dance with.

After the show is over, the showgirls, now in street clothes, come down and join Glenn and me at a table. They are beautiful. One, especially. She is model quality. Her name is Karol. I dance with her for a while and watch others watch her move. Later I take a photo of her for my "Disco Babes of Cusco" collection.

Glenn doesn't dance. Glenn tells me he never dances. But he's sitting there with this girl, looking like he's having a very fine time indeed.

On the way home he tells me that people kept asking if I was his father. Glenn is a year younger than my oldest daughter, so I told him that I was certainly old enough to be his father. Nothing else was said about it.

*   *   *   *

We sit down at Ukukus for "a good feed." The place is small and colorfully decorated with fantastical masks. For about two dollars you get a salad bar, soup and an entré with vegetables and a mountains of potatoes. While we're waiting for the food to arrive, Glenn talks about his biking experiences. A friend who has ridden motorcycles over half the earth had told me about biking to Ollantaytambo with Glenn. "He drives like a mad man," he'd said. Glenn brags about how aggressively he drives and admits to more than a few broken bones from motorcycle accidents.

We talk a little about our families.   Glenn tells me that his father died when he was only four and his mother had married again, briefly, to an asshole. Nothing else was said about it.

Finally, a good feed under our belts, at ten thirty in the evening, Glenn and I set out for La Paz, Bolivia. The rain has stopped, but the roads are still wet.   I have brought along a bottle of cañzo that has had coca leaves soaking in it for over a week.   I figure if it's to be an all night drive, we'll need it.   Or at least I'll need it to stay awake and keep Glenn company.

The cab to his truck is so high that I almost need a ladder to climb into it.   The steering wheel is on the right side, so I presume this thing was imported either from Japan or England.   Considering that the big diesel engine is just beneath us, the ride is quiet.   It is also smooth, but it sways a bit.   Glenn explains that the cab is isolated by shocks and they need replacing, so we lean noticeably away from the curves.   But that's all right.   It's fun up here so high, and Glenn is driving faultlessly even if his steering wheel is on the wrong side.   He opens package of two cookies, offers me one and throws the wrapper over to the floor on my side.   As the trip progresses the trash piles up until I have to push it aside to find room for my feet.

The road is familiar.   It passes the little town of Tinta, where I had come to the wedding only two weeks earlier.   Glenn tells me that he was on this road just a week before and people had thrown so many rocks in the road that he finally had to turn around and go back to Cusco.   The rocks were there as part of a protest, he said, about the location of a road that was being built from Brazil to the Pacific. The locals wanted it to be close.

A few minutes later we spot a couple of rocks ahead in the road. "At's nothing," says Glenn, as he artfully dodges them and the cab does a double-sway.   "Probably just somethin rolled offa the hill."

But as we near the town of Sicuani, there are more and more rocks in our path.   At first Glenn continues to propel the truck through without slowing, driving with consummate skill. But then there are not only rocks in the road, but telephone poles, laid across, and Glenn has to slow down, sometimes even stop and wait for an approaching vehicle to wend its way through the narrow opening. It is obvious by now that these are not acid-dental blockades, and it's getting to be a little frightening. At least it is to me. But not to Glenn. He hurtles through, cursing and weaving like Tazio Nuvolari traversing oil slicks in the *Mille Miglia*.

"Sicuani'll be the end of it," he says.

"Why is that?"

"It's the last town in the Cusco District. They're the ones protesting."

We approach the lights of Sicuani. The road bypasses the town to the right. We're abreast the town and suddenly come upon a group of stopped trucks blocking the road.

"Shit!" says Glenn as he jams on the breaks. "We're blocked." He leaps out of the cab and strides up ahead to check things out. There must be seven or eight trucks stopped. The drivers and passengers are all outside, talking to each other and scratching their heads. In a moment Glenn comes back. "It's blocked solid. They're burning tires a hundred meters up the road. Wanta go see what's up?"

"Okay." I clamber down from the cab and we move on up the road past the trucks. Ahead we can see the tires burning in the middle of the road, a crowd of people around, firelight flickering on brown faces in shabby clothes.

One of the truck drivers tells us they're not going to let anyone through until tomorrow morning. A group of about eight people come up behind us, men, women and children. Glenn tells them that he has to get to La Paz by noon tomorrow. Is there another way around? No, they tell us, no other way around. They also warn us not to go up to the crowd and the burning tires alone. We might get hurt. But if we go with them we should be safe. So we integrate with these locals and move up to the scene of action. The road here is a minefield of rocks and telephone poles. On the side of the road old tires are stacked, ready fuel for the fires.

There are no police to be seen.

There must be a hundred or more people. It's not exactly festive, but they seem to be having a pretty good time, except for a few angry ones who glare at us. We approach some young boys sitting on the curb.

"Por que este?" asks Glenn. What's the reason?

"No passas hasta mañana," the boy informs us.

"Ya, ya, no passas, but why? *Por Que?"*

The boy shakes his head. *"No passas hasta mañana."*

"Fuck!" says Glenn. "I'VE GOT TO GET TO LA PAZ BY NOON TOMORROW! I'VE GOT A BUNCHA FUCKING TOURISTS WAITING FOR ME!"

It's obvious that this ragged crowd couldn't care less about his tourists. We go back to the cluster of trucks and Glenn is still raging.

"Well," I say, if you can't do anything about it, you might as well chill out. We can sleep in the back of the truck until morning, then you can call."

But then a teenage boy approaches us. Dirty, torn clothes, muddy sandals. He says he will show us a way around for *una propina...* a tip. Without asking what the tip amount might be, Glenn agrees. No trucks have pulled up behind us so far, so we can still back up, turn around and take the other route. The boy takes his bicycle to another truck and asks the driver to load it. He is in a hurry, seems to sense danger for himself. I can just imagine what might happen if the angry members of that crowd up ahead caught him helping gringos around their roadblock.

Glenn is already backing the truck and turning. In a few moments the boy jumps into the cab with us and I am squeezed to the hump in the center... the engine cover. He asks for a flashlight. His voice is frantic. We head back a few yards and the boy has us turn into the streets of the town, then immediately tells Glenn to turn off his headlights.

We hurtle through the town with the boy shouting repeated directions, "left, straight, right." From time to time it is impossible to see where we are going without headlights, but the moment they are on, the boy issues the order to shut them off and then leans out the cab window pointing the flashlight beam just ahead of us.

The town, at least the outskirts we are careening through, is deserted. There are few streetlights, the houses and *tiendas* are two-story adobe, and the roads are dirt. We get through the urban area and come to an open field where the road becomes deeply rutted and muddy. Over to the right a half-mile or so we can see the tires burning on the main road.

We come to a turnoff that drops down and to the right. A little Toyota is trying to back out of this turnoff. We stop and the boy and Glenn descend to check out the situation. They start walking down the road and when my curiosity gets the best of me, I get out and start to follow them. The Toyota is still sitting there with the engine shut down. I slog through twenty or thirty yards and here come Glenn and the boy.

"What's going on?"

"Little log bridge," says Glenn. "Guy in the car was too chicken to try it. We're gonna show him."

But we have to lead and we are blocking the Toyota. We all remount the truck and Glenn backs up to give the car room. The car backs up, then pulls out of the way to give us room to plunge into the muddy road. Then the Toyota tentatively fool-lows us. The truck is slipping and sliding down the road and suddenly there is the bridge.

The bridge! I had expected logs laid transversely across beams. Nothing nearly so sophisticated. The bridge is six eucalyptus logs laid longitudinally across the water, two groups of three logs with a nice gap between them. Glenn guns the engine and aims the truck. "Don't slow down!" he shouts, presumably to both himself and the trailing car.

We make it across. The Toyota decides not to follow. Fifty yards later we come to more river, this time with no bridge. It looks shallow enough to ford and we proceed to do just that, slipping and sliding, and then leap up the opposite bank with a sickening lurch and bounce. We continue to climb with more slipping and sliding toward the highway that we have detoured. If there is a road or a path beneath us, I cannot detect it.

Finally we are at the highway. Behind us we can see the glow of the tire fires. The boy, more nervous than ever, tells us that the road should be clear from here on. We ask him about the amount of the *propina*. He indicates that he only wants enough to buy some new clothes, obviously a real need. Glenn reaches behind his seat and comes up with a South American Tours T-shirt. Obviously, this is inadequate, so Glenn also hands him a $10 bill. But the boy keeps gesturing at his clothes, pulling on his raggedy collar and showing the holes in his pants. Glenn ends up giving him another ten. The boy gets out and waves goodbye.

Pavement under our wheels... finally. We take a collective breath and aim for Bolivia. Less than five minutes later our headlights pick up another barricade. Rocks all over the road and a telephone pole that covers all but about three feet of roadway. There are four or five kids standing amidst the barricade waving their arms for us to stop.

"FUCK YOU!" shouts Glenn. He drops into a lower gear, speeds up, dodging the rocks and suddenly throws the right side wheels up onto the curb. There is a terrible crashing as we run over rocks. The kids run like hell. In a couple of seconds it's over. We are back on clear road again, both of us laughing hysterically.

NOW it should be clear. We are almost out of the *Departamento de Cusco*.

But no such luck. Another few minutes and we en-counter more rocks in the road and more kids. There are no telephone poles this time, but neither is there a curb to leap up onto. Walls of earth rise on each side. Without missing a beat, Glenn slams the truck to a halt and leaps down from the cab.

NOW Glenn dances. He starts kicking rocks aside to clear a path, first with his left foot and then with his right. What he can't kick aside, he picks up and throws aside. The kids, hands outstretched for the *propina*, offer to help. Glenn gives them a few coins and within about three minutes a path is cleared.

On our way again, Glenn says, "Arrr SHIT! There was shit on one of those rocks. I'll bet they put it there on purpose. The little bastards. They'll have the same rocks back in the road in five minutes." He drives using his elbow to keep the stuff off the steering wheel. A few minutes later he spies standing water by the side of the road and stops to wash his hands.

The barricades were finally past us. We could settle down and enjoy the trip. I pulled out the bottle of coca/cañazo and we each had a good swig. Everything is *tranquillo*.

We stopped in Puno around 4:00 AM. Glenn needed to pay a

hostal there where his tourists had spent a night.   It had been about 20 years since I had been in Puno.   All I remembered was a dark dirt street or two and a few buildings.   Now it was almost a city.   Glenn paid the bill and we struck out around the border of Lake Titicaca.

Titicaca is really an inland sea and the highest navigable lake in the world.   It is a place of mystery and lore.   The Incas claim that their first ancestors rose from Titicaca after the world had been in darkness.   The water level has risen and fallen over the years as the glaciers to the north have thawed and frozen.   An archaeological team recently found evidence of underwater structures in the lake. South of the lake is Tiawanaku, the ancient site that some believe to be over ten thousand years old.   There are mollusks found in Lake Titicaca that only occur elsewhere in the oceans.   Some believe that Titicaca was at sea level during civilized man's tenure on earth, that it raised suddenly through some awful cataclysm.   South of La Paz is a place called "The valley of the moon," a place of extreme erosion like that seen in southern Utah.   I had visited there 20 years ago and was told by a friend that a great mass of water cascaded through this land to cause the jagged spires all around.   It fits.

All the barricades behind us, we drive along the rim of the lake. It is first light; all is graphite gray, mountains rise beyond the water. The lake is smooth except for little patches of totora reed rising above the surface.   As the light strengthens, the totora reed boats can be seen floating upon the lake along with what appear to be little lateen rigged boats with bright blue sails.   The blue sails are new to me, the reed boats nearly as old as man in these parts.   All is beautiful and peaceful. Glenn presses on through the dawn.

Got to get to La Paz by noon.

We get to Desaguadero a little before six A.M.   The town is named for the river that delineates the Peruvian/Bolivian border.   The Desaguadero ("the drain") carries water from Lake Titicaca down to the smaller Lake Poopo.   The town is alive with activity but we discover that the border won't open until eight AM.   We take another slug of cañazo. Glenn leans his seat back to rest and I get out to savor the ambiance of this border town.

Just in front of the truck is a juice cart. Two men in blue uniforms are talking to the proprietor of the juice cart. There is a glass of something that looks like papaya juice sitting front and center . I ask about it and the uniformed men tell me it is "Maca." They use finger language to explain its virtues. The Andean Viagra. Fine. I buy a glass and raise it to my lips. It's scalding hot. I almost drop the glass and they all get a good laugh.

.

I wander around the Peru side of Desaguadero feeling very loose and fine if not fired up by Maca for sex. After a couple of hours we go through Peruvian customs and finally pass on over to Bolivia. Immediately the attitude seems different. The soldiers here are hardly a friendly lot. I remember the last time I was in this country my friend told me never to look them in the eyes. I remember that this is the country where they shot Che Guevara.

holds La Paz. It used to be that all of La Paz was down at the bottom of the bowl. Now it has spread up to the rim and spilt over. All red brick and tin roofs. We wind down into the bowl. Glenn is like a horse nearing the stable after a long ride. When we get into town he replays his Mad Max act. He's driving the beast furiously, yelling and diving into the midst of lesser vehicles, just daring them try to stop him. At one point a kid gets in his way and I think he's going to run the kid down.

But we finally get to The Copacabana Hostal without killing anybody. Glenn has phoned ahead for a reservation for me. (Richard... he doesn't know my last name any more than I know his.) I check into my room and come back looking for Glenn to thank him and say goodbye. But he's taking a shower. While I'm waiting I ask for another room. Mine is on the front, just above a very noisy street, and I have plans for sleeping all day. They move me back to another room. Its only window opens into the hostal's central open area. It is three flights of stairs up from the lobby and the single-sized bed takes up sixty- percent of the room. But that's all right. I'm exhausted from lack of sleep and lack of oxygen at this absurd altitude and I'm glad to have a quiet place to spend the day sleeping.

But first, I want to see Glenn. I go back into the lobby and ask about him. I'm told he's out at the truck. I go out, and there he is. He's had his shower and his yellow hair is flying wild. He's standing in the truck catching loaded backpacks that someone below is pitching up to him. He is shouting and flailing his wet hair this way and that as he catches the bags and tosses them into the interior of the truck. He seems not in the least tired or sleepy.

I wave to him. "Thanks, Glenn. It's been.... memorable."

He catches a sack, pauses for a moment and waves. "See you next year...Dad."

And he's back at it, shouting for more bags, catching and tossing, catching and tossing. Wild hair flying.

See you next year old son.

After a day and night's sleep I went to Tiawanaku the next day. Whatever its archaeological interest, it is a barren site and the ruins have been ruinously reconstructed. I'll take Machu Picchu, Ollantaytambo, Sacsahuaman or Pisac any day.

I flew back to Cusco.

CHRISTMAS IN CUSCO

The chalk marks started going down on the street in the afternoon of December 23rd. There had been a light rain, a gentle, no-thunder kind of rain that seemed to have no other purpose than to clean the streets. The sun came out around five, blessing us with just enough for a quick glimpse before it ducked behind the mountains to settle down into the sack. There were men and boys and a few women bent over marking out their little patches of territory with the chalk. The chalked territories were amorphous, amoeba-like.

The *campesinos* had come to town for the big Christmas market. I had begun to see them in the streets the day before. *Campesinos* are easy to spot because they are the faded people. Sun and dirt has faded their clothes so that the skirts and sweaters and pants and blouses are of colors so muted they are near to desaturation. Aside from a few baseball caps, they wear medium-brim felt hats the color of mouse fur. Their hats are all bent into different shapes; pork pie, peaked, pinched and whimsical. Nothing rakish, mind you. No cants or slants, pretty much straight on with at the most a brim turned up in the Annie Hall fashion.

By eight-thirty that evening, the plaza was teeming with *campesinos*. They were setting up their stands and tarps, unpacking their wares and settling in for the night. One man had even brought a fold-up iron bed, which he settled onto with a blanket. Traffic was snaking through the amoeba territories like canoes trying to traverse a river clogged with water hyacinths.

I watched from Duffy's balcony. There were family groupings, each with their sacks, beige and tattered, stuffed with things to sell. A few tourists wended their way through, but mostly is was the country people. Just below the balcony I spied a little girl looking at me. She was maybe ten and a little brother was nestled beside her amidst their sacks. They were both wearing the felt hats, both Annie Hall fashion. Their mother perched amidst other sacks a scant two feet away. The little girl smiled at me and I smiled back.

She had very red lips. I have never seen a little *campesino* girl wearing lipstick, so I guess it was a natural feature. Red lips and big white teeth that were still in her head. She moved her mouth as if she was talking. I pantomimed a response. Then we started making faces at each other, tongues and all. Her mother spotted this little interaction and issued a mild no-no. Still, we managed to steal a few surreptitious funny faces.

I went inside for a while. I sat with Duffy and he told me what a major pain in the ass these people were. They didn't really have any place to stay, and they certainly didn't have a place to make the necessaries, so they were using the streets as toilet. They especially liked the street next to Duffy's Place, and his clients had to traverse fifteen feet of the street to get to his bar.

Duffy said, "I went down and asked a female cop about the portable toilets that were there last year, and why weren't they here this year." He mimicked the cop, a señorita cop. "Oh weeelllll, I'll have to look into that." All very nonchalant and mañana. And Duff said, "Well will you get on with it. Look what they're doing to the street. Look what they're doing to the church. They've got no respect. It's sacrilegious! They're pissing on the church. And if you don't care about the Spanish version of God, look what's on the other side of the street... one of the remaining Inca walls in Cusco. Think about your heritage, for God's sakes. Get those porta potties in here before the desecration overwhelms us all. *Before we're buried in SHIT!"*

Making my own mind movie, I can just imagine this event, . Not before, not after, but exactly concurrent with the final period on his final sentence, Duff whirls about so fast that his two foot long pigtail lashes his shoulder. And then he charges off, his prominent chin, his Bob Hope nose and his Baseball cap bill forking the way ahead of him.

The back bar was empty. There's a TV in there, and I had a rare urge to have a look at the news. I used the remote to tune to CNN. It was horrible. All the people that had hated each other forever and ever were continuing to wreak havoc upon each other with whatever means seemed the most efficient. I turned it off and sat there pondering hatred and murder and war and theft and all such nasty things the uncompassionate of our species can conjure. It started to rain. It was a gentle rain, a rain with the quality of mercy. Rain always lifts my spirits. As long as it's not too hard or too long and I'm able to shield myself from it. Rain washes away the dirt. God's shower. Go to Lima and you get an idea of what a city without rain is like. I thought about all those dirt encrusted *paisanos* out there and gave my head a little nod. The kind of nod that says, "Yeah, that seems right, the rain."

I headed past Duff in the front bar on my way back to the balcony to see how the country folk were handling the rain. "It's raining," I said.

"Maybe it'll wash those filthy *campesinos* who're using my street as a toilet."

* * * *

You would never know it, but two rivers run right through Cusco: the Tullumayo and the Huatanay, also called the Sapi. (In Cusco, both streets and rivers change names with regularity.) These two rivers rush through two gorges on either side of the old city. They meet somewhere south of the city to form an acute triangle. By the time of the conquest, the rivers had been canalized so that they wouldn't inundate the city when the big rains came. But the Spanish, spotting prime real estate, covered the rivers and built houses over them. When the Incas were still in power, these two rivers swept Cusco clean day by day. Within a few years of the conquest, the rivers were clogged sewers. Cusco hygiene has never been the same. I read a story in a 1911 edition of *The National Geographic* about a woman's trip to Cusco. She said the only place on earth that smelled worse was Calcutta. Even when I first came in 1975 Cusco was a little on the pungent side. It has improved a whole lot since then... except for times like Christmas.

* * * *

I left Duffy's Place around 12:30, an unusually early hour for me. Beneath the balcony was a nest of *campesinos*. They were lying beside, around and over each other in a tangle of humanity, all tranquil, all apparently asleep. As I neared the corner, two boys approached me, said "*buenas nochas*," and shook my hand. No request for a handout. I was astonished. I *expect* to be asked for a handout. I bought a bag of chocolate covered peanuts at the only remaining tricycle mart on the street. I opened the bag, had a couple of balls of candy and headed home. The candy must have been bait. They now began approaching me with outstretched hands, this time palm up. I doled out my candy, two pieces at a time, until the candy and the *campesinos* were gone.

The next day, the day before Christmas, the Plaza de Armas was a massive tangle of vendors. It was raining off and on, and much of the tangle was covered with those godawful cheap neon-blue tarps that must be everywhere in the world by now. I just wish they'd made them green or white. I wanted to buy a few gifts for kids I expected to see at Charlie's house where I was going for Christmas dinner. So I plunged into the swarming crowd.

Ever since Thanksgiving, I had been particularly thank-ful for being here. The merchant assault, North American Style, was blissfully absent. Very few Christmas decorations are displayed until around the 20th of December. I don't mind the decorations at home so much, but I've about gotten to the point where if I hear one more time "Jingle Bells," or "Santa Claus is Coming to Town," or "Rudolph the Red-Nosed Reindeer", I'll rip the cone out of the speaker with my bare hands. Yes, after years and years of it, I have become sickened over the cheapening of what should be a joyous and thankful celebration. Just give me a rendering of Handel's "Messiah" and forget about giving so much stuff, thank you. I prefer giving presents at unexpected times.

Well, it looks to me now that all that month-long shop-ping that goes on in the US is crammed into one day here in Cusco. You cannot imagine the diversity of STUFF that was available for sale on and around the Plaza: Religious and non-religious ceramic figu-rines, moss and grass and enclosures for nativity scenes, corn husk figures of tooth pulling and baby birthing, sweaters, scarves, socks, blouses, trousers, knit caps, felt and straw hats, furry animals made of alpaca, ceramic figurines of couples having sex in every position imaginable and a whole bunch of other things that I couldn't iden-tify. The far end of the plaza was the food section with stand after stand cooking the same skewers of *anticucho* and potatoes, baskets of tamales covered with cloth to keep them warm, juice stands, *chilé rellenos*.... damn near everything except the traditional Andean dish, cuy.. guinea pig.

And for these thousands of people the city sanitation department had brought in three portable toilets, each of them located over a grilled opening to the sewers below. It was hardly adequate. (Charlie told me of going to mass Christmas day and having to hold his nose entering the cathedral.)

I bought a cute little Koala bear on the plaza, but that was it. After so much struggling through the crowd, sometimes waiting minutes for a long stream of humanity to pass through a one-way opening, I gave up and walked up the street where you could move with relative freedom. I bought a double rotor helicopter that, only too late, I discovered, made horrible blaring and screeching sounds as it crawled around the floor, its blades whirling and lights flashing and figures of people inside nodding back and forth. I also bought, for the toddler, a toy earthmover.   And thus ended my Christmas Shopping.   Relatively easy, I'd say.

The market was closed at midnight and by Christmas morning the SELIP street cleaning crews, dressed in their orange overalls, orange hats and orange masks, bustling like a colony of ants, had the Plaza back to its normal pristine self.

I had a fabulous Christmas day dinner at Charlie and Betty's house, gave presents to the kids, and through it all, missed my own children just a little bit more than I do on every other day of the year.

ON BECOMING A CUSCO GURU

Nikolai, my friend and occasional instructor in Spanish, showed up at Norton Rat's Tavern tonight. I hadn't seen him for several days. I asked his friends about him and they told me that his mother said he had gone in search of his "earlier religion."

"What? " I asked. "Catholicism? Mormonism? Seventh Day Adventist?"

They had no answer.

Niko had always seemed to me to be a relatively bal-anced person. He was studying for a degree in chemistry, drinking reason-ably and regularly, and enduring the vicissitudes of life imposed by the raging hormones of a man in his twenties. He is a tall, broad-shouldered good-natured and good-looking guy.

When he appeared tonight there was something different about him. He was thinner. He seemed high on something or other and he was mildly raving. He threw his arms around me and told me how much he'd missed me. He sat at the bar beside me and ordered a beer. "I'm such a fool," he kept saying.

"Why are you such a fool, Niko?" I asked it over and over but all he did was hang his head low over the bar and repeat the same words: "I'm such a fool."

Niko's English is on a par with my Spanish, so we have to struggle a bit to get through to each other.

"Why are you such a fool, Niko?"

He holds out his fingers. His fingers are long and thin, the fingers of a piano player. One of them has a small scar on it. "Look at this finger," he says.

"What happened?"

He was building a rock dwelling somewhere way up in the mountains, at an elevation of 4,000 meters and this big rock fell on his fingers. It was swollen up like a grapefruit until he got down to a civilized altitude and found a physician who injected his fingers with antibiotics. Antibiotics work for everything in South America, and you can buy them as easily as aspirin in pharmacies everywhere.

Niko is talking up a storm. It's interesting to watch him talk. He has a wide mouth and when he speaks his lower lip moves more than his upper lip. It opens up the bottom part of his mouth. I always thought that mode looked pretty elegant.

"Is that why you feel like a fool, Niko?"

"Yes. I feel like a fool."

Niko seems like he's on coke. Everything about him is exaggerated. Or maybe he's just been drinking a lot and, having never seen him really loaded, I don't have a frame of reference

for his altered-consciousness behavior-patterns.

Niko was definitely exhibiting altered-consciousness behavior-patterns.

"Why are you feeling like such a fool, Niko?"

"I feel like such a fool."

"Because a rock fell on your finger? What were you doing building a rock house up there at 4,000 meters ?"

Turns out it was a back-to-the roots-Inca thing. I have a lot of respect for that urge. My altered friend Niko, moaning over his foolishness, had been on a mission to connect with those Inca roots, and like many Inca rituals, it took place at a very high altitude. I guess to the Incas it seemed that the higher you go, the closer you are to the ultimate father, to *Inti*, the sun. It's why they sacrificed children there, why there are annual pilgrimages even today to the glacial heights of the Andes.

After a beer, Niko calms down a bit and suggests that we play darts. Actually, he didn't suggest it, he simply extended a fistful of darts and told me we were going to play.

We played and he won. But it was only by a tiny margin, a fact I attribute more to his inebriation than any sudden grasp of the game that had flowered in me.

We went back to the bar and his head drooped even lower.

"Niko," I say, *"Vale la Pena?"* Was it worth the pain, the experience you had?

He lights up for the first time in the night. "Oh, yes!"

"You gained a better understanding of your culture."

He prefaces with the rudiments of his genealogy. "I'm only part Peruvian," he says. "My father was Argentinean. My Grandfather was Greek. Papadiamantopoulus is my middle name."

"Well did the Peruvian part of you get some enlightenment?".

One of the reasons I can talk to Niko is because, even though his English is not much better than my Spanish, he speaks distinctly. At least he speaks distinctly to me. He has that wide Greek mouth and it stretches and arches and protrudes in perfect O's and he places his tongue perfectly in his oral cavity. Listen-ing to Niko, I feel that I almost understand Spanish.

Niko answers my question. "I was raised mostly in Cusco," he says. "But I was born in Argentina and they, the Argentineans, look down on the people of the Andes. They think of them as ignorant mountain people. That's what my father always said. 'They are barbarians,' he would say. When I was very young, when he was telling me good night at my bed, he would tell me that shit. What he was telling me was that my mother was a barbarian and he was civilized."

"Ooohhh," I said.

"Let me finish," he said. "This set up a great conflict in my spirit. Am I half barbarian? Am I five-tenths uncivilized? I felt that there was something I needed to understand about half of myself."

"And you found it?"

"I found something....I found *Pachamama*, the mother earth, and I found *Inti*, the Sun. The mother earth, the receptacle of seeds, the womb of our survival. And I found the father, the energy that comes from the Sun, the father God."

"How does this religious epiphany make you feel about your studies in the science of chemistry?"

"It makes me totally aware of the perfect order of *Pachamama* and *Inti*."

"That should make you feel good."

"It makes me feel wonderful," he said.

"Okay. You're alive, aren't you? Maybe you've got a bruised finger, but is that a big deal considering what you gained? What are you complaining about?"

"I am so stupid," he says.

I'm beginning to think that this has nothing to do with his injured finger.

"I need to talk to a friend," he says. "You are my friend, Richard."

"*Sin duda*, Niko. I am your friend." It's true. I like this guy. He is earnest, he is intelligent, he has a goal. He tries to teach me Spanish. He is also, as mentioned earlier, in thrall to his gonads. Niko admitted to me a few months ago that he had failed a class in chemistry because he had bedded his teacher, who later had seen him with another girl.

Oh yes. Early twenties.

"My heart is broken," he tells me.

Then I get the truth from him. Niko had just seen his true love, the woman he has loved since first sight, has always believed would be his perfect wife... had seen her with another man. He was devastated.

"I need to talk to someone about this, Richard. I need to talk to someone old."

I make a mental note to explain to Niko that he should in the future, for the sake of diplomacy and sensitivity, substitute the word "wise" for "old." .

Then I think about all the pain I have felt in the past over lost love.

"It takes time," I said.

"How long?"

"Somewhere between two weeks and two years, I'd guess."

His head went lower. His forehead was only inches from the bar. I thought he was pondering the possibility of a two-year sentence to brokenhearted misery. So I was relieved when he said, "Will you buy me a drink, Richard?"

"Of course."

He got a bottle of beer to cry into. Oh, he was so miserable. I envied him, in a way. I envied him the capacity to feel anything to such an extreme: Extreme joy, extreme fear, extreme pain. (As long as it's not physical... As Oscar Wilde said, "Lord spare me the physical pain and I'll handle the mental." Or something like that.)

On the other hand, I thought of the Zen teachings. The whole business of removing yourself. Try to look at life as though you were watching a movie. Stand back. Try to see the humor in it.

I tried that for years and began to feel bored with it all. What is the purpose of my being here? Is it to remove myself from here? I remember Profi's lecture. The guru-bashing lecture.

I have no answers. Maybe I need to be even older. Or maybe I could just pretend that I know the answers. But, God, I have such a low opinion of anyone claiming to know the truth, claiming to be a bridge to God. The Priests, the Shamans, they have been around forever, interposing themselves between the deity and us.

On the other hand, I may be losing a wonderful opportunity here.

THE BIG FANTASY

Maybe I could become a Guru!

Like Pinochet or Rimpoche. I could have an infinity of Rolls Royce's. Rich, nubile and innocent young virgins would give me their inheritances and their cherries. Vast congregations of seekers of all ages from all walks of life would give me undying devotion and other offerings.

Gurus and shamans are big business here in Cusco. Think of all those people who think God is going to land at Machu Picchu or Sacsahuaman in a space ship and carry all the true believers off to the Promised Land. They are ripe for the picking.

The seekers so ready to take San Pedro or Hayahuasca, throw up, hallucinate, and find the true meaning of life.

After all, I have the credentials. I have white hair and could grow a white beard and I have the age to pull it off. My grandfather was a Presbyterian minister. I have been a stage actor with some success. I'll bet I could have them eating out of my hand. Or rather placing treasure into my hand.

Maybe if I made a few image changes:

I need to change my clothes. I need to lose the jeans and get some pants that look like pajamas. I need to buy some embroidered, gauzy shirts. Maybe now and then on special occasions, a long flowing robe of saffron....No...white! I need longer hair. Hair that is blow-dried to place the curls and straights just so. I need to recall a few of the right phrases..."Free yourself from the shackles of life" and "Be here now." Things like that. Thoughts that Henry Miller called, "All that falderal that blows out of the East like a breath of the Plague." (I don't feel quite that way...just enough to love the quote.)

And therein lies the rub.

I would have to be more cynical to pull it off. I'm too much of a country boy. Cynical is alien to me. I don't mean to sound like Mr. do-goody or anything like that. But I cannot for the life of me use my white hair and advanced age to ravish virgins... even non-virgins. Hell, even old dowagers. It's another character flaw.

Oh, If only I had a little more Jimmy Swaggert, a little more Jim Bakker in me.

I could be so rich, so Rolls Royced, so righteously screwed.

* * * *

Enough of that fantasy. Back to the present. Poor Niko. His head is now touching the bar. He is groaning in emotional pain. "She was the perfect one for me, Richard. Perfect in every way. But she wanted someone with money. I have no money."

That was pretty obvious, considering he had to ask me to buy a drink for him.

"I need to talk to you Richard. Can we talk? I need someone old to talk to. You've been through it all. Maybe you can help me."

There goes that "old" again. If he can't say "wise", he could at least say "older."

On the other hand, watching poor Niko in his torment and misery, sobbing into his suds, I am comforted by an old song from the movie *Gigi*. Maurice Chevalier, in his old prime sang it...

I'm so glad I'm not young anymore.

PARURO

For about a year now Yheni has been telling me about this little town several hours from Cusco. She has a grandfather and an aunt and uncle living there. Her uncle is convinced there is gold on his property and Yheni wanted me to bring a metal detector down from the States so we could do a little prospecting.

I forgot all about the metal detector but another reason came up to visit Paruro. One of Yheni's nephews was graduating from lower school and he wanted her boy friend René to be his godfather. They asked me to come along and take pictures. They also suggested that I bring a sleeping bag.

On the appointed day I packed clothes and cameras, rented a sleeping bag and met René and Yheni at the bus station. We boarded and I squeezed into a seat that made airplane seats look like Barca-Loungers. A rather large man sat next to me and unfolded his newspaper. René and Yheni sat together in the seats in front of me. Their 3-year-old son Jan sat in René's lap. There were no empty seats on the bus. Others were carrying children in their laps. One man was even carrying a large television set in his lap.

As the crow flies, Paruro is about 50 kilometers from Cusco. But the trip by bus takes nearly two and a half hours. As we start out of town a young man stands at the front of the bus facing the passengers. He is a magician... the first I have seen in Cusco. He begins his spiel as the bus lurches around braking and accelerating and swaying left and right, forcing him to reach in every direction for support. He is a short man, thin, probably in his early twenties. He trills his rs with a flourish. He is bright and engaging. Throughout this lurching and braking he manages to pull off a few standard tricks with moderately adept prestidigitation. Most of the passengers ignore him or watch without enthusiasm. I applaud him. I remember my days on the stage and how much approval means to a performer. I also appreciate it that he is doing something different. When he has run through his repertoire, he pulls out a bag of candy and tells us that he will be handing pieces to each passenger. If they don't want it, they can give it back. If they do want it they can give him a little money. I give him a little money. A few miles afterward the bus stops and he disembarks.

We climb higher out of Cusco, which at 11,500 feet is already pretty high. The road is dirt. The scenery is magnificent. The mountains are green and gentle. There are clusters of Eucalyptus trees here and there, but mostly we are traversing rolling, open spaces. For a few miles out of Cusco screes of garbage running down the side of hills mar the scenery. This is the Cusco dump.

The large man sitting next to me is still reading his news-paper. He is like my Siamese twin. We are so close that we are joined from shoulder to knee. It felt a little strange at first, but after a while it was all right. Here was I, a gringo, pressing flesh with a total stranger, a Peruvian, and it was just fine. That, I suppose is a cultural effect of living in close quarters. It feels pretty human.

Jan has his arms around René and is facing me. We make faces at each other. Jan has only recently become com-fortable with me. I was at their house, sitting on a stool going through René's CD collection, when Jan comes over, stands stock-still a foot or two away and looks at me unflinchingly for a couple of minutes. No sound, no change of expression, just eyes wide open. That did it. The next thing I know, he wants me to play with him.

(René told me later, that Jan does the same thing to him, that stock-still unflinching staring at close range. He and I agree that no other kid we have encountered has done that.)

I alternate between terror and amazement.   The bus swings through curves that border thousand foot drop-offs with no barricade, none of those comforting steel fences designed to prevent catastrophe. I am in a window seat and I snatch breath looking down, down, down a thousand feet into flat farmland.

Six months ago I had rented an apartment from a Spanish couple. I left for a few days to go to Ollantaytambo. When I returned, my apartment had been commandeered. There were young people standing around with wounded bodies and dazed expressions. It was a group of Spaniards on tour who had been in a bus accident. The bus had run into a patch of rain-soaked road that didn't hold. The bus had fallen, had careened down the mountainside. Two had been killed. Others were in the hospital. Those who were here were bloody, bandaged and shocked.

This is what I thought about as we rounded the curves, our wheels no more than a foot from that precipitous edge. The fact that this was the rainy season was just so much more to amplify my anxiety.

But the vista! Unbroken it was, like Colorado. You could see forever over the rolling hills, verdant and soft with here and there a cluster of trees, an isolated farm of adobe habitations and barns with cows and horses grazing.

It was isolation. Humans had not cluttered the land.

We climbed and climbed, cresting at 14,000 feet. Looking around for 360 degrees you could see the entire earth. The soft green hills ranged to the horizon.

It was ironic, being wedged into this narrow seat in con-summate constriction with my Siamese twin, and at the same time looking out the window to free and expansive earth. I could feel this stranger's body pressed against mine and at the same time embrace such a big part of the world. It was such a fine duality. It made my spirit soar. It made my heart sing.

Mostly the trip was a curling over mountain roads of dirt, switchbacking through this uninhabited piece of upthrust earth. But now and then there was an isolated habitation of adobe dwellings, fences and animals. There were more horses than I was used to seeing. And the horses appeared stronger and larger than the mangy critters typical of this part of the world.

After about an hour of unbearably gorgeous scenery and unbearable constriction from the seats, we stopped at the little town of Yaurisque, which is apparently a regular stop on the route. Immediately the bus was surrounded by women offering an extensive menu of take-out meals. . Proffered to my window were plates of trout, potatoes and vegetables. Yheni left the bus for a few moments and came back with three plastic bags, each containing one chile relleno and a couple of small potatoes.

The bus pulled out and we dug into our bags. The Chile Rellenos were so nice. Green Peppers filled with a mix of vegetables and meat. The potatoes were just potatoes. God I get sick of potatoes here. Potatoes for appetizers, potatoes in the soup, *papas fritas* along with the main dish. I have yet to encounter a potato dessert. However that may simply be a gap in my ex-posure to the culture. But you have to remember.....

The Andes is the home of potatoes. When people think of potatoes they usually think of Ireland and the Potato Famine. Here's the truth of the matter. When the Spanish conquered Peru with its nonpareil agriculture and its hundreds of varieties of the noble potato tuber, they brought back to Europe only one strain. That one strain got into Ireland and enabled a massive population explosion. The people of the Andes had thrived on the potato for thousands of years. If the blight got into one strain of their tuber, there were many more to take their place. The Irish had no such insurance. They had only one strain. And when the blight hit their strain, the food that had fueled their population explosion vanished. Much blame is rightly laid upon the absen-tee landlords, those rich fops living the high life in England, who gave not a thought to their tenants. But the root of the problem was a lack of genetic diversity. It was agricultural, more than political, incorrectness.

As an interesting sidelight...I read recently that the coca leaf helps to metabolize starch. It explains in part how a man could work all day on a stomach full of potatoes and a cheek full of coca.

After our lunch stop, at Yaurisque, an altitudinal dip in our journey, we began climbing again to another stretch of rolling, open, verdant mountains, over roads of dirt snaking around the hills with sheer drops on one side or another. Isolation after isolation.

Yheni turns around to face me and explains how this Cusco-Paruro bus system came into being. It seems that a resident of Paruro won a goodly amount of money in the lottery. With an exhibition of insight and intelligence rare in lottery winners, this man bought two busses and established the Cusco-Paruro bus line. Turns out it was a good investment. The busses run twice a day and they are always full. This lottery winner has linked an outpost with the ancient Inca capitol and it has worked very well for him and for the people of Paruro. It has worked so well that he has added a couple of combis... vans, we would call them... to his fleet. This is the only post-lottery-win success I have ever heard of. The man should be a national hero. Hell, the man should be a global hero.

Two hours and fifteen minutes after leaving Cusco, we get our first glimpse of Paruro. Way below us in a valley, it is. A cluster of terracotta buildings nestled in the arms of three converging rivers.

We are entering the town. We are not yet to the main plaza when Yheni signals the bus driver to stop. He does so, and we disembark. Standing on the side of the muddy street is a very thin man who is wearing leather shoes, gray slacks, a cardigan vest of lighter gray and a white shirt. He seems oddly out of place here, not only for his garb, which is far from indigenous, but also for his physical appearance. He looks Vietnamese. But he is not. This is Juan, Yheni's uncle, a teacher of high school mathematics. He welcomes us and we are led up the street to his place.

His place is a complex of adobe buildings, some of them very old, some not yet finished. We are taken to a small room where we may leave our things. The room has one bare light bulb hanging from the ceiling. There is a desk, a bed and a bookshelf recessed into the adobe that is largely occupied by math texts. The floor is packed dirt.

I meet Juan's wife Teófila and a few of their eight children. Many of the names in Peru are strange to me. Names like Friné and Yahira and Faridé. But Juan and Teófila have come up with a few dillies.

The names of the children are:

Jhon	(A European spelling for Juan, and pronounced Yawn, like René & Yheni's son.)
Hernan	(DeSoto?)
Rocio	(dew)
Joseph	(That guy with the virgin)
Azucena	(White Lily)
Alain	(Originally intended to be "Alan" for then president Alan Garcia, but Teófila didn't like Garcia, so they inserted an "i".)
Vetner	(named for the writer Julio Vetner)
	And finally and most confusingly:
Jaivith	(A sort of anagram made from the names of the older children: J from John, A form Alain, V from Vetner and ITH, I don't know.)

The preponderant image from both parents and children is one of politeness and reticence. We are invited in to the main room, another separate adobe structure that serves as kitchen, dining and living room as well as guinea pig quarters.

Along one wall is a guinea pig condominium, three tiers tall. The cages are raised off the ground about a foot, and there, underneath their caged brethren, many un-caged guinea pigs huddle.

The house, they tell me, is over a hundred years old. It is curious, seeing these well dressed, polite people living in such primitive surroundings. But a new wing is in progress and will be finished when they can get the money. So far there are adobe walls and a roof, but it has stopped there. In a burst of mathe-matical whimsy, one of the rooms has been constructed in the shape of a trapezoid.

René, Yheni, Jan and I are offered seats at the only table. We are given Mate de Coca, the tea made from coca leaves. It is a drink that would be illegal in the US; perhaps in the rest of the world, but here it is like tea to the English. Waiting for the meal, I take pictures. I walk outside and see a little boy of about six leaning against the wall. He is so shy I have trouble getting him to look at me. I ask him his name. His answer sounds like "David," but with something twisted. Later I find out that this is Jaivith. I make friends with this shy little boy on the spot. He is a sweet kid.

It is time for the meal. I had been told, warned maybe, that we were to have cuy, which is Quechua for the little rodent we call "guinea pig." Cuy is bedrock, indigenous, Inca food and being a culinary coward, I have never attempted it. (There is, by the way, a painting of the last supper in the Cathedral of Cusco where everyone is eating cuy.)

I am full of fear and loathing. The plate is placed on the table. The little critter is stretched out before me, all brown and furless. His toothsome mouth is wide open as if in a scream. His little feet reach out to me. I watch Yheni for guidance on proper cuy consumption. It is a hands-on indelicate operation. Yheni tears off a leg and pulls back skin to reveal meat.

With her first bite, there is a great, fearful, defiant squealing and chattering among the living guinea pigs. They know. Surely they know.

We the guests are the only ones honored with cuy and a table whereupon to eat it.   The rest of the family sit quietly, plates on laps, eating a simpler rice and potato fare. Now, contemplating this roasted rodent before me, I would gladly change places with them. But I screw my courage to the sticking place and attack.

I clutch at the roasted hide and pull it back to reveal a pale meat. I struggle with fork to lift it.   The live guinea pigs squeal in protest, but I fight on. I finally get some of this flesh into my mouth and begin chewing. It's tough, but not bad.   I think I can do this. Yheni is way ahead of me. She has delved into the critter's innards and is eating something that looks like paté. She tells me that the intestines have been removed, but the liver and heart remain.   But what is that squishy black stuff that looks like something half digested? I can't handle it. I manage a little more of my cuy's meat and desist. I eat a little of the mass of potatoes that accompany the cuy and then quit, giving the excuse that I am trying to lose weight.

Yheni keeps eating until nothing but bones, claws and head remain.   I congratulate her on her courage.

Afterwards, we go outside.   I ask Juan about the gold.   He tells me he suspects it is right there in his little yard.   There is, he says a swath of land running through this area where Inca gold is buried. But now is not the time to look for it.   The time is when the rains are over;   when the earth is dry.   I tell him I will try to come back in August with a metal detector.

Now it is time for us to head for the school where Juan teaches mathematics.   There is a party for the students who have just graduated from the 6th grade and are poised go on to a higher level.

We walk down the main street of Paruro. René, a Dutchman, and I, an American, are the only Gringos in sight. We must be the only Gringos that have been in Paruro for twenty years. People gawk at us as though we each had two heads.

There are supposedly about seven thousand people living here, but the feeling is that of a near deserted town.   There are very few people in sight. I ask Jaivith and his friend to pose for a picture. Later I slip them each a piece of the magician's candy.

We walk on. I am struck by the fact that no one has tried to sell me anything.

"Not too many tourists in Paruro, are there?" I ask Juan in my miserable Spanish.

He just shakes his head and laughs. What an absurd idea, tourists in Paruro.

There are no hotels here and just a few restaurants. And as I found out later, no cold beer. None. Not a one anywhere in the town. If I were to cite one complaint about Paruro, this would be it.

We climbed a hill to the school. On the right there were about five big, blue tractors with harrows and plows scattered around. They were behind a fence and appeared to be in long disuse. I asked about this and Yheni explained.

The tractors had been given to the town by the Fujimori government. They were Japanese tractors. They had been used for a while, but now the people couldn't get parts for them, either because they didn't have the money or because all commerce with Japan was now forbidden. Fujimori, having raided the treasury went on the lam to Japan. Peru wanted him back to stand trial but Japan would not extradite the former president to Peru.

So the farmers, and most of the people here were farmers, went back to the old ways. The old one-man wooden plows that had been in use for thousands of years, and the cattle drawn plow that was more modern. I wonder about the real reason for the disuse of those tractors. I think maybe it is that people are slow, slow, slow to change their ways. And if the tractors were used, fewer people would be needed in the fields and then what would they do? It's an old, old conundrum.

* * * *

The School Party. It didn't look like much of a party. The big room was ringed with school seat/desks filled with boys of eleven, twelve, maybe thirteen years. They were well behaved, but joyous.

A man in a floppy felt hat was going around the room serving chicha, the fermented corn-based beer. They told us it was non-alcoholic, but we wondered... how can anything fermented be non-alcoholic? Were they getting the kids lubricated?

They sang some songs and then someone put a CD into a boom box and they got up and danced. Yheni danced with one of her nephews for a while and then we left. On the way out I took off my straw hat and made a sweeping bow. The boys all laughed and cheered.

Now we went to Paruro's Plaza de Armas, sat on a bench and watched. There wasn't much to watch. The feeling was still of desertion. But then we heard music and out of one of the side streets a small procession appeared. They were carrying placards and chanting something I couldn't understand. Yheni explained it to me. They were marching for sanitation. *Marching for sanitation!* What a concept. The town was engaged in a consciousness-raising effort. We drink this water, so let's keep it clean. Later someone handed me a leaflet promoting toilet hygiene. (The toilets here are usually just a slab of cement with footholds and a hole over a deep pit.) I translate loosely.

USE THE TOILET PROPERLY

1. Pour water into it before you use it.
2. Do your business into the hole.
3. Put the paper you use into the box you will find in the bathroom.
4. Pour water into the hole after you finish.
5. Wash your hands before leaving.
6. This process will help to keep infections away from your children.
   Good for those people of Paruro who care.

Later, about seven of us, including Juan and Jaivith went to dinner. We sat at a long table and ate meals of rice, potatoes and a fried egg. I ordered meat with my meal. It came out looking like a huge tongue. I think it was beef... or maybe alpaca. It was tough and more than I could eat even if it were tender. I cut it up and passed it around. And I gave away at least half of my rice and potatoes.

I paid for the meals. The bill was 19 sols... $6.09 U.S. for all seven of us.

There was, as I said, no hotel in the town. But there was a close approximation. It was a community building that had rooms with beds that were available for a few sols per person. At nine in the evening, Yheni, René and Jan went to bed. Going to bed at nine is, for me, a huge waste. I love the night. I could hear revelry down in the town, but I was leery of joining a bunch of drunks as the only Gringo. So I took my sleeping bag and went outside. I found a reasonably dark place and lay down to look at the stars with my binoculars. The sky was patchy with clouds for a while and finally was completely covered. I lay there for some time, telling myself that I should lie under the night sky more often. It lifts my spirit.

I heard a noise. It was a small family of pigs. They snuffled and shuffled by me no more than three feet away. After a while it began to drizzle, so I gathered my things and went inside.

Still not ready to retire I knocked on the half open door of the concierge's room. Earlier, I had noticed a large wooden harp there. The concierge was lying on his bed listening to music.   I asked him to play the harp. He struggled up from the bed, grinned, nodded, and scratched his head. He sat down with the harp, and without tuning it began to play.. He apparently knew only one tune, for he played it over and over and over again. His repertory was small and his talent even smaller, but he was authentic. He was authentic like just about everything in this isolated little farming community. Everything but the tractors. And those onerous things were now caged and ineffectual.

Juan has eight, count 'em _eight_ children, and Juan, being an educator, wants his children to be educated.   I wonder, what does education do to a youngster who lives in a place this isolated? Education is what will enable an escape from the one-man plow. It will enable an escape from cutting grain with a scythe or running a tiny shop that barely supports a family.

Paruro has a few television sets here and there, supposedly only two telephones in the town, and no Internet connection. At least no Internet connection so far. But one of Juan's nephews is working on a satellite connection. Give the kids of Paruro video games and a World Wide Web access and things are bound to change.

I envision a scenario where the educated children leave Paruro and the streets become even more deserted, and adobe buildings, long unused, crumble into dust until Paruro is almost a ghost town with only a few elderly hangers-on hanging on.

Or maybe another scenario. Those educated young people go out into the world and see that the gentleness of human interaction they knew at home is not out there everywhere. And maybe they'll come back and improve the lot of their fellow citizens and somehow retain the beauty of the life they had. Maybe even do it with tractors.

That's a tough order.

But Juan wants to educate his children. For better or worse. That's why he wants to look for gold. It's probably the only way he'll be able to manage it.

Maybe at some later time, after the rains have ceased and the ground is dry, I will come back with a metal detector and see if we can find some gold on Juan's property so he can finish his house and educate his eight children. When you think that most of the gold the Spanish took either ended up at the bottom of the ocean or was used to finance losing wars, using what little is left for education sounds like a pretty good idea.

EL SEÑOR DE LOS TEMBLORES

Photo by Walquer Zamora
Cusco

Throughout its long history, Cusco has been periodically rocked by earthquakes. The Inca builders were acutely aware of such likelihood and constructed their walls and cities accord-ingly. The walls of stones so perfectly fitted, are battered, meaning that they lean in as they rise. The Spanish, long wedded to the plumb line and mortared masonry, built their walls to an exact vertical. The results were, and still are, predictable: When the temblors come, the Spanish walls collapse and the old Inca walls remain standing.

One might think the Spanish would learn from ex-perience and emulate the construction practices of the Incas, but such was not the case. The Spanish came up with another ingenious solution to the problem. Here's how it happened:

In the year 1650, there was a terrible earthquake that leveled most of the Spanish buildings. The aftershocks continued for days until someone finally came up with the brilliant idea of taking this life-sized effigy of Christ on the cross out of the Cathedral and parading it about the city on a litter. And lo and behold, it worked. The aftershocks ceased.

Seeing in this an obvious cause-effect relationship, the yearly procession of *El Señor de los Temblores* was born. It continues to this day, every Monday before Easter Sunday. It is apparently the most important day of the year for the people of Cusco. It is more important even than Christmas. It is a very, very big deal.

Early in the afternoon, soldiers and school children, all in their uniforms, stand at attention facing the great door of the great cathe-dral. Television cameras are set up on tripods and scaffolds, even on booms. An air of expectancy hangs over the Plaza de Armas. A Mercedes sedan, perhaps the only one I have seen in Cusco and most likely the carriage of the Bishop of Cusco, is parked beside the Cathe-dral. In some years the streets are decorated with artful designs in flowers arranged upon the cobblestones. Traffic is rerouted and the traffic police in their white pith helmets trill noisily on their whistles.

Then, a little before four in the afternoon, the bells in the cathedral begin to peal. How many of them there are, I do not know, but included in the chorus is the bell known as Maria Angola, reputedly the largest bell on the entire continent. When Maria Angola is struck, its deep, ghostly, sonorous groan sup-posedly can be heard from forty kilometers away.

The faithful citizens of Cusco begin streaming toward the square in an inexorable surge of humanity. This is the most important day of the year, even more important than Easter itself, for one's luck for the entire year to come is set irrevocably on this day. This is so because at the end of the procession, just before the Christ figure is returned to its place in the cathedral, it is blessed by the bishop of Cusco, *and unless you want rotten luck for a year, you had better be there to witness the event.*

For a crowd-draw, no political candidate can touch the procession and blessing of *El Señor de los Temblores*. The Plaza de Armas is so tightly packed with bodies that any one of those individuals could relax completely and still remain standing, supported by his neighbors.

At four in the afternoon, *El Señor de los Temblores* emerges from the Cathedral, borne by a score of litter bearers. Swaying tassels hang from the ends of the cross. For ages, votive candles have been lit below the figure of Christ so that it has turned black. The television cameras roll, broadcasting the spectacle to the entire nation.

For the next few hours *El Señor de los Temblores* is borne around the city. From Norton Rat's Tavern we observe, sometimes from the balcony, sometimes from the television. Shortly after dark the procession crawls down the street just below us, makes a left turn and proceeds to the Cathedral door. The all-important blessing is given and *El Señor de los Temblores* is returned to his place inside the cathedral..

Then it is over and the bodies begin to stream out. Looking down from above, we can see streams of people filing through the throng like blood flowing through arteries. As the Plaza empties, the street cleaners take over with their dustpans and whisk brooms, cleaning the debris and raising a great cloud of dust.

We return to the bar, nearer the tap to be, and order up another round. After a while Jim calls us over to the window. There is a man standing stock-still on the broad apron that fronts the Cathedral. "He's been standing there like that for ten minutes," says Jim.

I note the time on my watch.

The man is wearing a knee length jacket and is bare-headed. If this were Venice, California, he would surely be a street mime. Jim and Doug and I go out on the balcony to observe. Fifteen minutes later the man is still rooted. His head is bowed slightly and rain drips from his scraggly beard. My first thought was that he was drunk, but after watching for a while, I change my mind. I don't think a drunk man could stand so still, so rock-steady, for so long.

There are others standing at the great door to the cathe-dral, facing it, heads bowed in prayer, almost touching the door. When one leaves, another takes his place. They try to keep candles lit in the rain. It is all very quiet and reverential. It seems another manifestation of the power of this event in the minds and hearts of the people of Cusco.

Suddenly there is movement from the still man. He rocks ever so slightly from one leg to the other. There is no forward movement, only left to right. He rocks back and forth five times. Then he is still again.

"I think he's seen God," says Doug.

"Most likely the Virgin Mary," says Jim. "In South America there is no God, only the Holy Mother."

"Whatever, something's gripping him."

He begins to rock again. It's been thirty minutes since we started watching the man, and there is still no forward movement. Then, after rocking back and forth a few times, he takes a few tentative steps forward. He is headed for the steps, twelve of which there are just ahead of him. We make bets on how long it will take him to reach the steps. I feel a little base, betting on the actions of a man who is seeing God...or the Virgin... Whoever.

He keeps moving like this. A few side to side sways, as though in preparation, then a step or two forward, then still again. Forty-five minutes after our timing had begun, he reaches the stairs. Then he stops.

"Maybe he has some nerve disorder, says Doug."

"Maybe he's just not in a hurry," says Jim.

I can't stand it any longer, this watching from a distance. I want to see the man up close, so I leave the balcony, go down to the plaza, climb the steps to the Cathedral and pass close by him. I learn little. He looks to be in his fifties. His clothes are patchy, but they aren't rags. His face is blank, not the startled blank of ecstasy, just plain blank. Whatever sort of ecstasy is gripping the man, it is not evident on the surface.

I return to the balcony and report my not-so-news.

We are beginning to loose interest. This is like watch-ing a tree grow. But then... once more... there is movement. He is stan-ding at the edge of the steps, has been standing there as if hesitating, but now he rocks left and right.

I'm afraid for him, afraid he is going to fall. I have this urge to go and take his hand. But I don't.

"Wanta bet on whether he falls or not?" says Doug.

"Maybe we ought to go help him," I say.

"What!" says Jim. "And ruin his ecstasy!"

"Maybe falling down the steps is part of the plan," says Doug. "Something like the Stations of the Cross."

He rocks again, and then, miraculously, carefully, he descends one step.

"The twelve step program," says Doug.

Which reminds me that I want a drink. But I can't bear to tear myself away from this excitement. It's thrilling... unbear-ably suspenseful. *He is going down the steps.*

I open the door and yell to the barman, Joel to bring me a Ricardito, a mix of vodka, grapefruit juice and tonic water; a drink designed by and named for myself.

One by one the man descends the steps. He pauses long on each, and before each step down, he rocks. The descent takes more than half an hour.

Now comes the really risky part. Getting across the street. It's difficult enough for *me* to get across the street that surrounds the Plaza, what with taxis aiming at you, accelerating as if to nail you before you make successful passage. But for a semi-catatonic person in the throes of some kind of ecstasy, it is a crapshoot.

Doug's kindness gets the best of him. He goes down to the man and asks him if he is alright. The man says yes and Doug asks him where he is going. The man says he is going to his hostal.

When Doug returns he tells us this and says, "Going to his

hostal is significant. It means he doesn't live here. He's here for *Semana Santa*... Holy Week."

He was across the street and moving slowly down the sidewalk when we finally lost interest. It had been two hours since we first began our vigil. It was an amazing exhibition of just how intensely affected are these people by the Procession of *El Señor de los Temblores*.

*   *   *   *

The next year I got another take on the spectacle. I have been in Cusco for maybe four of these processions and have al-ways watched from the safety of Norton Rat's Tavern. But this time I left my hostal a little too late. Hundreds of the faithful were hurrying toward the plaza and I joined them. As we got closer, the crowd thickened until there was only a small stream of people headed in the same direction as myself. Then the stream became a trickle that finally stopped about ten feet from the entrance to Norton's. It was impossible to go any farther. I tried once or twice to force my way through the cluster of bodies, but it was out of the question. People would look at me and shake their heads. Were I claustrophobic, I would have panicked. Fortunately I am not claustrophobic, and fortunately I am taller than most Peruvians by nearly a head, so I could see and breathe.

The Black Christ entered the Plaza and began to make his way at an excruciatingly slow pace toward the cathedral. There were occasional stops that seemed interminable. Beside me, below me, a young mother, scrunched in the press of bodies, unable to see anything but legs and torsos, looked up at me. Now and then she would lift her child over her head to see the procession. Somewhere down there, another child was clutching at my pants, frighteningly close to my crotch. I was beginning to sweat. Babies were beginning to cry and the Black Christ crept on, its tassels waving in stately rhythm. The smell of the pressed bodies became stronger. Behind the litter, people jockeyed to get near enough to touch the sacred thing. It crossed my mind that now would be a perfect time for an earthquake. God always has a custard pie up his sleeve, but he didn't throw it today.

With all the speed of a tranquilized slug, the procession approached the great door of the great cathedral. It faced this way and dipped, then that way and dipped, until the four corners of the plaza had been saluted. There was, I suppose, the customary blessing from the Bishop of Cusco, but I could neither see nor hear it. Finally the great door opened. There was applause. Police cars on the other side of the Plaza flashed their red and blue lights. The Black Christ crept back into the cathedral.

And the crowd began to move. At least parts of it began to move. My part was as packed and motionless as ever. Just a few feet from Norton's entrance and I was stuck. Another ten minutes and a stream of young boys began pushing their way through. I slipped into the stream and was carried by it to the steps, down the steps, a left turn so that now the door to Norton's was visible. I was almost there. Then somehow, the stream began rushing like the inexorable waters of the Urubamba River in spring. I was being swept past the door, helpless. Then, like the appearance of an angel of salvation, a hand reached out to me from the doorway. The hand and its arm belonged to a beautiful young girl. I took her hand and she pulled me out of that rushing river of humanity into the relative safety of the doorway. I thanked her and staggered up the steps and into Norton's. I was badly shaken, but unharmed. I ordered a drink and went out to the balcony to watch the scene below. The Plaza was still packed with people struggling to exit. It was another thirty minutes before the population had dwindled to manageable proportions. The street cleaners began their work, sweeping up the litter into dustpans with their whiskbrooms, sending up clouds of dust that began to fill my nostrils. I went back in, sat at the bar with friends and ordered another drink.

The Incas loved a procession. In olden times, once a year, the

*mummies of the Inca Kings of yore would be taken from their palaces
and paraded around the plaza.*

*The rituals and rites of the Incas were the most elaborate and
rigid to be found in the pre-Columbian Americas. Or maybe anywhere
in the world. Around Cusco there were somewhere between 330 and
400 sacred places called "Huacas." They were situated along 42
sacred pathways called "Ceque lines." Each of the Huacas required
specific sacrifices at specific times to be attended to by a specific
noble family.*

*The Spanish conquerors were determined to convert these
heathen Indians to their religion. The True Religion. That was their*
raison d'etre. *There had to be some excuse for the rape and pillage of
this empire. So in the name of the True God, they set out to destroy
the sacred places of the Incas. And they used every obscene measure
imaginable to separate the people from their pagan ways.*

*"You are heathens," said the Spanish. "You worship rocks and
waterfalls and you carve stones into strange shapes and worship them
too. Know this, you pagan infidels, there is only one God. And we
know his name."*

*Well, the change wasn't too hard for these pagan in-fidels.
Not only were they used to being told what was true about earthly
matters, they were used to being told what was true about gods. It
made for easy transitions.*

*Huacas forbidden? No problem, we'll pray to your saints.
One group of deities is as good as another as long as we've got
bunch of them.*

*And Christ? We know about Christ , but we called him by
another name. The old legends told us about the creator god,
Viracocha, and his son who returned to earth in human form. He was
a white man with a beard and he wore a long, white robe. He brought
with him a message of peace and love.*

And the Holy Ghost... that's easy... God is everywhere. Everyone knows that.

No more mummy processions? No problem....

We have El Senor de los Temblores. *And we parade him around the plaza on a litter carried by a dozen men.*

Just... as in olden times... did we carry our king... who was the one and only... the true earthly representative of God?

The Inca... Our king...

The son of the Sun.

BRICHERA

When my friend Gary bought Paddy Flaherty's Bar, I had to go over and wish him luck. Gary owns a couple of buildings, a café and a bar. And lately he's become my landlord. Gary's a very tall, thin Irishman with bushy eyebrows and a long, loping stride. He's a familiar figure here, glimpsed occasionally like flashes of lightening as he moves between his various establishments. I suspect Gary must wear out at least one pair of shoes a month making his rounds.

While I was talking to Gary, another gringo came in. He sat down right in the middle of the bar and ordered a Bourbon and water. When his drink was served he glanced up and down the bar. I raised my glass to him and we drank. After about five minutes I hopped down off my perch and went over to him. I would never do this in the States, but for some reason, it seems natural here in Cusco.

I stuck out a hand and announced my name. "Mind if I join you?"

"Glad to have the company. I'm Ron Strickland."

Ron was on the short side… about five seven, I'd guess. He was a little overweight and looked close to my age. He had a pleasant, guileless face and a defenseless smile. I was ready to like him on the spot.

I mounted the stool next to him. "What brings you to Cusco?"

"I needed to go someplace different," he said. He had a southern drawl that sounded very close to home.

"Where are you from Ron?"

"High Point, North Carolina. Ever heard of it?"

I laughed. "Charlotte," I said.

"No kidding? Well, how about that!"

We shook hands again.

"Where'd you go to school?" he said.

"Chapel Hill"

"I'm damned! More coincidence. Me too. Graduated in Business Admin in 73."

That was more than a decade after my time, so there was no way we would have known each other there. "Let me guess," I said. "Business Administration... High Point. You must be in the furniture business."

"Was. I had a little factory that made institutional furniture. Mostly stuff for schools. I just sold the business."

"Retired, hunh?"

"I guess you'd call it that. I'm trying to figure out what to do next."

"Family?"

"Two sons. Grown and out on their own. My wife died about a year ago."

"I'm sorry."

"Thanks. That's why I sold the business. Seemed like I needed a turnover."

"And that's why you're here?"

"Pretty much. I've been all over Europe and some of Asia. I wanted to do something really different."

I had gotten a lot of this man's story in a hurry. He must have been doing quite well with that little furniture business to have done all that traveling. Or maybe he was selling desks in Europe and Asia. There was nothing ostentatious about Ron. He was wearing khakis and a polo shirt. His watch, I was glad to notice, was not a Rolex, but a Timex. He was wearing brown wingtips, a strange sight in Cusco, if you don't count the bureaucracy.

"Different," I said. "Well this place is different. How long have you been here? How long're you staying?"

"Just got in two days ago. I don't know how long I'm staying. So far I like it."

Never one to miss an opening, I launched into my Cusco Chamber of Commerce mode, telling him probably more than he was ready to digest about the town. We ordered more drinks and began to glow. I learned more and more about Ron Strickland. He seemed strikingly decent, a church-going, upstanding, philan-thropic citizen. As the night went on he got a little tipsy and started talking about his wife. They had been married just out of high school and had been that rarity, a happy, devoted couple. After she died, something inside him seemed to die, and he was out trying to restore his life. He started using a phrase I loathe and despise.

"When you get to be an old feller like me..."

After about the third of these self-defeating pronounce-ments, I touched his forearm. "Ron," I said, "I'm about ten years older than you. Please don't say that around me. If you're an old feller, where does that put me? Damn near the grave, I guess."

He gave me a puzzled look that quickly dissolved into a smile. "By god, you're right!" He banged his glass down on the table and spilled some of his drink. The barman rushed over with a towel.

"Another drink," said Ron. "*Por Favor Señior.*" He started laughing. He continued laughing until he was dangerous-ly near tears. "*OLD FELLER?* Well fuck that!" He caught him-self and put his open palm to his mouth. "Pardon my French. I don't usually talk like that."

"It's okay here. You're not in church."

He looked at me, his eyes shining with tears of laughter and relief. "I don't *have* to be an old feller, do I?"

"Not yet, anyway." I remembered a long-ago birthday party that my oldest daughter organized. This is what her invi-tations said.

It's Richard's 49th. But don't tell him. He doesn't know it.

"It seems like a lot of it's attitude."

Ron is Thunderstruck. "Yes!" He banged his glass on the bar again, spilling more bourbon. Once again, the barman was on the spot with the towel. "Uh Oh," he mumbled. "I think it's time for me to go home. I'm embarrassing myself."

"Don't worry about it. Probably the altitude. It affects people that way."

"You're not drunk."

"I'm used to it. And I'm not drinking bourbon."

"I thought all good Tar Heels drank bourbon."

"That's where I started, but I sure can't do it anymore."

He pointed at my glass. "What's that, gin?"

"Good God no. That stuff kills me worse than bourbon. This is Vodka."

He eased carefully off his seat. "Hm. Vodka. Good idea." He motioned for the check. When it came, he laughed. "This can't be right." He produced a pocket calculator and figured the exchange rate.

I looked at it. "That's right," I said. "Five wild turkeys at 9 sols each. Seem like too much to you?" No wonder the guy was unsteady. Five 100 proof Wild Turkeys would have put me way under the table.

"Too much! Do you know what this would have cost in High Point?"

"A lot more."

"A whole hell of a lot more. This is ridiculous." He paid the bill and left a huge tip.

"Vodka's even cheaper," I said.

"I'm gonna think about that." He weaved a little.

I was worried about him. "Let me go down with you and make sure you get a safe taxi."

"No, no. I can walk back to the hotel."

"I know you *can* walk, but it's not a good idea at night. Especially after you've been drinking. If there are thieves out there looking for easy prey, the flashing light points down to a drunk, whitehaired gringo."

It was difficult for Ron, the former CEO of what I suspected was a fairly substantial private enterprise, to take orders from anyone else. But as part of his new life he left the old ways behind him and said, "Okay." There are about twenty steps from the bar down to the street level. Ron clutched at the railing and took his time. "I'm gonna think about that vodka," he said. "I don't like feeling this way."

We went out to the street and I hailed a taxi for him... one that had a yellow sign on top with official taxi numbers on it. "Where are you staying, Ron?"

"Let me see....something about a monastery."

"Monasterio," I said. "Ron, that place is outrageously expensive. It's about the most expensive hotel in town."

"I can afford it."

"Good for you. But do you *need* it?"

"Need it? Whadaya mean?"

"This isn't Paris, Ron. If you want to stay in Cusco for a while, let me take you around to a few other nice, comfortable hotels that cost a tenth as much and are a lot closer to the reality of this town. Save Monasterio for the fancy nights."

"Fancy nights?" The words schlurped out of his mouth.

I opened the cab door for him and bent down to speak to the driver. *"Monasterio. Tres sols, no mas."*

Again, Ron says, "Fancy nights?"

"When you've got a *brichera*."

I closed the door and shook Ron's hand through the window. "Hey," he said. "Are you gonna be in the bar to-morrow night?"

"Want to meet for a drink?"

"I don't want to impose," he said, "But I need someone like you to show me the ropes."

"Glad to do it. At least I'll show you the ropes I know."

As the cab pulled away, Ron leaned out the window waving at me.

"What's a *brichera*?" he shouted. Then he was gone.

As I watched him go, I thought about all the earlier times when I'd been walked down steps and installed in a safe cab. It made me feel like a graduate.

The next night Ron showed up at the bar around nine. He was wearing a shirt he had bought at one of the local handi-craft shops. He had dropped the wing-tips for hiking boots and he was wearing a cap that had a coca leaf on it. Ron was sliding right in.

He came down to the end of the bar where I was sitting and pulled up a stool.

"How's it going, Ron?"

"Great, great!" He ordered a vodka tonic. "I went shopping today." He indicated the shirt and the cap. "Whadaya think?"

"Good one. You're wearing in well. Good one on the vodka, too."

"I'm sorry about last night. I hate getting drunk in public."

"I hate getting drunk anywhere, but there are times.....too many times. And I couldn't drink five Wild Turkeys and remain standing."

"Thanks," said Ron. "That makes me feel better. We Tar Heels can hold our likker."

I told him about a college drinking survey that was conducted by a popular men's magazine of the time. The University of N.C. at Chapel Hill was excluded from the survey. The reason given was that this was an amateur ranking and our alma mater was considered professional. Ron looked extremely pleased at that bit of lore. He took delivery of his vodka tonic and raised his glass. "Cheers. Here's to the pros."

It was the beginning of a friendship. I liked Ron and he liked me. We were both straight shooters. We were both Tar Heels. We were both white hairs.

Ron let his Cusco days roll by without a thought to moving on. As time went on, it seemed that I somehow had become his confessor. It's like that with me. Something about me makes people feel comfortable opening up. I think it's because I don't have eyebrows. I look defenseless. Also, I'm a pretty good listener.

"Something's changing in me," said Ron. He stumbled around with "uh's" and "ah's." and finally found his words. "I still grieve for Helen, but.....I don't think I've told you much about Helen, have I?"

I shook my head.

Ron fiddled with his drink. He started to say something, then didn't. He looked directly at me at me for a moment. His face was guileless, vulnerable. He looked down into his glass and let one big laugh erupt. "I don't usually talk about things like this." He took a deep breath. "Helen was what you might call highly sexed. You know, on our first date we got to first base. After that first date, right away we got to second base, then third base. Godamighty! Real fast, you know. We had the major hots for each other. But the funny thing is, we didn't hit that home run until after we were married. You know what I mean?"

I nodded. He took a gulp of his vodka and then gave me a funny sort of look.

"Then, after we were married, I had to run hard to keep up with that girl. Seemed like if a day went by without us...you know... it would ruin her health or our relationship or something. I started taking multivitamins. I found out about that Brazilian Root... Yohimbe... and I started taking that.

"It took me a while, but I finally got into her stride." He shot me a proud and satisfied grin. "It was wonderful. Oh, my God, it was something else." He was shaking his head and chuckling. Then he sort of caught himself. "Oh, after a while we cut down a bit. Cut down from maybe eight or nine times a week to maybe six or seven. Helen was one wonderful nympho-maniac. It got better and better, and we never got tired of it. You would think that after a while you'd get tired of it, but that's not what happened. We'd keep finding new ways to connect."

He took another gulp and then coughed, spewing vodka. "Oh, I don't mean weird stuff. Just, you know, subtle things that... I don't usually talk like this, but it's something I need to talk to someone about. Okay, subtle things. Like the tiny signals that came from inside. From the inside where we were connect-ing. It was..." He shook his head and there were tears in his eyes. "It was something else. It was really something else."

Neither of us said anything for a while. He looked away from me and brushed his eyes with his sleeve. Then he looked at me. "You know what I mean?"

I thought back and nodded. "Yeah."

"But for thirty years?"

"No," I said.

He hung his head over the bar and shook it slowly. "It's getting to me. You know, you get used to something like that and it's hard when it's not there. You know what I mean?"

"So what are you gonna do, Ron?"

More of the hangdog, slowly shaking head. "It's been over a year. At first I didn't think about it. I was just too busted up, you know. But lately it's been creeping back up on me."

We were sitting at the bar. He touched my elbow. "I need some fresh air," he said. Want to join me on the balcony?"

So we went out onto the balcony. We were loosened. We had the balcony to ourselves. We didn't talk for a while. We just watched the scene below.

There was a gringo standing on the sidewalk obviously waiting for someone. Every couple of minutes he would look at his watch. He had graying hair, looked to be mid-forties and cut a fine figure except for the anxiety.

I pointed him out to Ron. "Watch this. I'll bet he's waiting for his date. I have a feeling it's a local girl."

"What gives you that feeling?"

"Just wait and watch."

The guy began to pace. Twenty yards this way and a glance at his watch. Twenty yards back and another glance at his watch. This humiliating ritual goes on for fifteen minutes.

"I feel his pain," says Ron.
"Yeah."

"Wanta bet on whether she shows?"

"Only if you'll let me bet she won't," I say.

"Yeah," says Ron.

Forty minutes later the guy kind of schlumped off, his sails sagging.

Ron and I both felt his pain.

"That's not unusual," I say. "Getting stood up. Not if they are local girls. She'll probably see him tomorrow, or even later tonight in the disco where he met her last night. She'll tell him she is so sorry but... something about her mother."

"Mother?"

"Yeah. It's always the mother, they say. But it's really about her two-year-old child that she's not gonna admit to any time soon."

Without comment, Ron puzzles this for a few moments. A scant few moments. Then Ron spots three girls crossing the square. Long thin legs clad in tight, bell-bottom jeans. They are walking in lock step.

We are both reverentially silent.

When they are out of sight, Ron fires off a brittle little laugh. "Wow!" he says. "Did you see that?"

"I love this plaza," I say.

Ron shakes his head and shivers like a washed horse throwing off water. "I've gotta do something about this." There is more head shaking, then he looks at me with that wide-open, desperately vulnerable look, and says to me:

"I'm scared. I'm really scared. Helen was the only woman I've had any real sexual experience with. I don't know if I can do it with anyone else." He takes a gulp of his drink, puts the glass down, pauses for a moment, then lifts his glass for another gulp. Then he repeats the process.

I say nothing.

Then finally, in a small, quiet voice, he says, "I'm scared shitless. Honestly, I don't know if I can get it up for anybody else after Helen. That woman could get me up even if when I was drunk. Helen just wouldn't take no for an answer."

" Maybe you need a re-entry program," I said. It was an inadvertent *double entendre.*

"Like what?"

"Well, let's think about this. Let's brainstorm. What are the ways?"

He looked at me like this was the first time he had come across the thought. "Well, maybe a prostitute? But the problem is, I don't think I could get it up for a stranger... a professional. Can you buy viagra in Cusco?"

I nodded. "Without a prescription."

"Hmmm. Do you know anything about those kinds of places here?"

"No," I said, "But I have contacts."

Now it so happened that I had been feeling derelict in my reportorial duties in not covering the whorehouse scene in Cusco. Well, it's a nasty job, but somebody's got to do it.

So then Ron and I, two white-haired gringos, enlist the aid of my knowledgeable friend and go off to what was promised to be the "best whorehouse in Cusco". We get there around midnight.

Thankfully it's not intimidating. Immediately inside the door is a dance floor. Two couples are dancing. Flanking the floor, left and right, are long benches. Upon them sit about fifteen pulchritudinous *putas*. Cusco's finest. Beyond the dance floor is a bar that seats maybe six people. Ron and I go to the bar and order drinks. Surprisingly, no one approaches us. We drink our drinks and try to look comfortable. Ron doesn't take long to actually get comfortable. Soon he nods to a very pretty girl at the other end of the bar. They get out on the floor and dance. Ron is sort of awkward, but the girl doesn't seem to mind at all. She's making all the right moves. She's wearing this wonderfully sexy white garment that's cut above to show a grand cleavage and parted below to reveal legs as fine and full as her breasts. It's easy to see she's arousing Ron from his long sleep of celibacy.

Another of the girls approaches me. She's not bad. Not the prize Ron's surrendering to, but nice enough. She starts hanging on me and hustling these very expensive drinks. When a drink is delivered and paid for, she is handed a chit that I assume is redeemable for cash at the end of the night. She's telling me how handsome I am. Even with my limited Spanish I understand her. Clearly, it's easier to understand words you want to hear. However, I have to ask her to repeat herself. Like most of us, I crave hearing compliments twice. I am so taken with all this flattery that I totally forget about my friend. A few minutes later, when I surface and look for him and his girl, they are nowhere to be seen. I get a little tweak of satisfaction, thinking of Ron embarking upon his re-entry.

My newfound ardent admirer suggests that we repair to private places. I'm not much for institutionalized dalliance, especially in a bed still warm from other bodies, so I decline and continue to buy these inordinately expensive drinks. The girl is blowing softly in my ear. I don't even think about the money. In the back of my hazy mind I am secure in the knowledge that If I run out of cash, I can borrow from Ron.

Every few minutes a boy comes through, mopping the floor with vigorous strokes. I don't think much about this until I spot another girl pouring her drink on the floor. Then I remem-bered what someone had told me about these places. The girls make their money having you buy drinks, but they don't want to get drunk themselves. I am about ready to call the game on the little hustler beside me, when I am interrupted by a tap on the shoulder. It is Ron and he doesn't look too happy.

Flat... expressionless, he says, "Can we go?"

"Okay," I say. I give the girl a kiss on the cheek and tell her some other time.

In the cab, Ron is silent. He is turned away from me, looking out his window. I leave him alone. We are almost to his hotel when he leans over to me to speak. He doesn't look at me, he just points his mouth in my direction and whispers.

"You know what the worst part was? I couldn't get it up for her. It was too cold, too professional. She just bounced around on me and faked an orgasm." He didn't say anything for a moment. He didn't move, either. Then he said, "It was a really bad imitation of a real orgasm. God, after Helen....she would start with this groan that seemed like it was coming from the bowels of the earth... and her toes would start curling." He shook his head. "I felt like I was playing in the wrong sandbox. I don't think I'm cut out to be whorehound."

"I understand. I'm not either."

The next night we met again at Norton's. Ron seemed to have recovered from last night's embarrassment. He was eyeing every girl that passed.

"Haven't given up hunh, Ron?"

"What do you mean?"

"Given up on girls."

"Oh no. Except there's a problem. I'm lusting for girls who're young enough to be my daughter. You know, back home girls stopped looking at me a long time ago. After a certain age, it was like I was invisible. But here, I keep getting these sly looks."

She sees a meal ticket, I'm thinking. I'm also thinking of the old saying: Men are drawn to beauty. Women are drawn to the wallet.

But I keep my counsel. "Well," I said, "Young girls are about all you see in this bar." It was a perfect opportunity, and I seized it. I launched into another historical lecture. I told him about the attitudes on virginity in Inca times. "See," I said. "The Inca sent his emissaries around the empire to seek out the cream of the crop. It was sort of like Cinderella except that the Inca king needed more than one. *Many* more than one. The thing was, they had to be virgins. So the parents, who needed the girls to help with the family chores, encouraged early deflowerment." I thought about this for a moment. "Maybe deflowerment isn't a real word, but you probably know what I mean... don't you Ron?"

But Ron wasn't listening.. He was watching a couple of girls who had just entered the bar. Actually, "watching" hardly covered it. Ron had spied a fine pair of bottoms and was laser locked to them. I understood. It was indeed a lovely scene, an undulating cannonade. The girls dipped out of sight into a booth and Ron turned to me with a strange look. It was like he had taken some kind of recreational drug that I didn't know about.

"What did you say?" said Ron.

"I can't remember."

"Did you see those girls?"

"Would I miss something like that?"

"Do you think they're prostitutes?"

I shook my head. "I doubt it. They're more likely *bricheras* than prostitutes."

"What's a *brichera*?"

I was trying to think of the best words to convey the meaning of *"brichera,"* but then Ron nudges me and nods his head in the far direction of the bar...where the girls are. He's getting flushed. His feathers are rustling. His tail is flailing about this way and that.

Yes, Ron is horny.

Ron is also nervous. He detours, chattering, "Did I ever tell you about my hobby? Woodworking. It's an antidote to making school desks for a living. I got into my business because I loved woodworking. You know?"

Ron is talking to me, but his eyes and his head are some-where else. Occasionally he flicks a glance in my direction just to let me know he knows I'm sitting right there beside him and listening. Just a flick, then his eyes go back to the prey, devouring.

"I have a woodworking shop you wouldn't believe. Every hand and power tool you'd ever need. I can miter, I can dovetail, I even learned, and it took me damn near forever to learn it, how to inlay."

Then, all of a sudden, he's no longer interested in his woodworking. He looks me right in the eye and says, "I'm going to buy those two girls a drink."

"Very good idea. I don't think anybody's ever done that in this town."

"Bought a girl a drink?"

"Bought a stranger across the room a drink."

"Well, do you think it's alright?"

"I think it'll knock 'em out. I'll pay for one of the drinks. Have you picked yours out yet?"

For a moment he seems offended. Then confused. Then he lights up with laughter. "You can have first choice."

"We're talking through our hats," I said. "You know as well as I do that if there's any deciding to be done, it will be done by the women."

So we call the barman Joel over and tell him we want to buy drinks for the two cute girls at the end of the bar. Whatever they want. Joel, suave as ever, nods with understanding. Like he has seen this maneuver a thousand times. But I can see a smidge of astonishment in the corners of his eyes.

The girls, of course, know what is going on. Girl radar is far more powerful than boy radar. Nevertheless, they make an excellent display of surprise when Joel asks for their order and gestures toward us. The girls light up. Ron sweeps his arm in invitation. The girls look at each other in elaborate confusion. Ron makes another sweep of his arm. The girls giggle a little and point to themselves. "Us???, they seem to be saying. Is this something about US????"

"What's going on?" says Ron.

"I don't know, but I think they expect us to come to them. Isn't that the way it's usually done?"

"I don't know. I've never done this before."

But Joel, who has seen Ron's gesture and knows who as paying the bill, sets the girls' drinks beside Ron and me. That Joel is no fool. The girls pretend not to notice, so I go down there and simply ask them if they would like to talk to us. That seems okay to them, so I suggest that we sit together. That seems okay to them as well, so we gather in a booth. Two girls on one side, Ron and me on the other.

Then it got hard. The girls didn't speak much English, I don't speak much Spanish, and Ron speaks none. At times like this, I find it best to make faces rather than to struggle with the language. Ron, who seems not much for making faces, hauls out this talking electronic translator. You type in something in English and it speaks it back to you in Spanish.

Ron typed in something, pressed a button and pointed the thing at the girls and it squawked, tinny and electronic, *"Como se llama?"*

The girls giggled, then answered. *"Soy Friné,"* said one. *"Soy Faridé,"* said the other. Thusly did Ron, Richard, Friné and Faridé commence our electronically facilitated social intercourse. The machine was a godsend. It greased the wheels of conversation like a pint of vodka. Most of the translations were laughable and that was all the better.

Ron was all charm, all lit up with enthusiasm. If he had ever hesitated over charming a girl thirty years younger than himself, he had certainly lost that hesitation tonight. It was the first time I had seen him so lively. As the night went on, his focus began to hold upon Friné, who was sitting diagonally across the table from him. She was all attention for Ron, smiling and making flirty little faces.

I got up to go to the bathroom. When I came back Friné had moved over to my seat to be closer to Ron. They were deep into it. I sat next to Faridé and we attempted conversation, but there wasn't much spark. On the other side of the booth it looked like the flame of love had been ignited. Ron and Friné were whispering and essaying tentative little touches.

After a while the girls got up and went to the bathroom. When they came back they announced that they had to go. Something about somebody's mother waiting for them.

Oh Boy.

Ron stood to say good-bye. He kissed both girls on the cheek, first Faridé, then Friné. He held on to Friné's hand for a moment, and a signal passed between them.

We went back to the bar and ordered more drinks. Ron was sort of glassy-eyed and didn't have a whole lot to say.

Finally he spoke. "That was really something else."

"What was really something else."

"I did something I haven't done in over thirty years. I asked a girl for a date."

"Yeah? What are you going to do?"

"Lunch tomorrow. I thought it would be the best place to start."

I wanted to remind Ron of the guy who paced and kept looking at his watch, but I didn't. I doubt he would have heard me anyway.

Those fears, at least, were not realized. The next night he showed up at the bar with something akin to a swagger.

"How was the date?"

He grinned and said. "Great."

"Tell me about it."

Ron sighed and grinned again. "I took her to the best restaurant I could find. She was all smiles. She kept touching my arm. I felt really good... like a teenager again. After lunch she wanted to go for a walk, wanted to show me the market. On the way we passed a clothing store she wanted to go into. She said there was a friend who worked there who owed her money and when she got the money she was going to buy some jeans. The friend wasn't there, so I offered to buy the jeans for her. I ended up buying two pairs of jeans and three blouses."

"*Brichera*," I said.

"What's that?" Ron said through his haze.

"A gringo chaser. A girl looking for a bridge to the USA. A guy doing the same thing is a *brichero*. It's one way for them to get out of here... hopefully to a better life."

The definition just waved over him. He was in his own head. Then he said, "There's more. But don't tell anybody else, Okay?"

"No way. We're fellow Tar Heels."

"I feel really stupid about this. After I bought her the jeans, she pulled me into the little dressing room and kissed me by way of thanks."

"Kissed you on the cheek?"

"Mouth."

"Tongues?"

He couldn't look at me. He just nodded.

"Then what?"

"I bought her a silver bracelet."

"That's okay, Ron. If you can afford the Monasterio, you can afford a silver bracelet. Besides, if you keep it up you might get laid."

"I want to change hotels," said Ron. "She asked me where I was staying. I didn't want to sound rich, so I told her I was in some little place near the center of town. Of course, I couldn't give her a name, so I just evaded. Now I've really got to find another place to stay. Can you help? A place where I can have company."

Ron was far from through.

The next day we went in search of more modest lodg-ings. He put me in charge of the search and pondered more important matters. "Can you buy viagra in Cusco?"

I didn't remind him that this was a question already answered. "You can buy just about any prescription drugs here without a prescription."

"She doesn't seem nearly ready yet, but I want to be prepared."

"Be sure and get some rubbers as well."

He looked at me as if offended.

"You don't want to be getting her pregnant."

"That would be impossible. I had a vasectomy years ago."

"You might want to keep that to yourself."

"Why?"

"She might be looking for a baby."

He thought about that for a while and we went on in silence. We set out to climb the steep hill of Cuesta San Blas, and Ron started huffing and puffing. "I don't think I want to get much farther away than this," he said. "Especially if it's more uphill." We stopped so Ron could catch his breath.

"We're about there," I said. I took him to a place I'd been staying at off and on for years, the Amaru Hostal. It's a family-run lodging that has rooms with private bathrooms and 24-hour hot water. The owners are nice, the help polite and honest. We got Ron a nice room with a view for $17 a night. Breakfast included.

We checked out his room. We stood at the window, looking out over the tiled rooftops and the intensely green mountains rising beyond. I don't think Ron saw the view. "Do you think they'll let me bring a girl in here?" he said.

"I remember seeing a sign once that said no unregistered visitors after midnight. The sign said it was for security reasons. But I imagine if you tip a little at the right times, you won't have a problem." I paused for effect. "Not at your age anyway."

He shot me a confused look, then, a beat later, caught on and laughed.

The next day I went to Ollantaytambo for a few days to see old friends and revel in the raw beauty of that incredible place. I should have known better than to leave Ron to his own devices. There was something different about him when I got back.

He came in to the bar with the vulnerability of a man who

wears no clothes. His eyes reminded me of someone accustomed to eyeglasses when he has removed them. It is not naivety, not stupidity, just what looks like a reckless exposure to danger… the danger of walking into a lamp post in one case; the danger of walking into the wiles of a very pretty and much younger woman in the case of my friend and fellow Tar Heel.

Ron was transported. He said, "She asked me, 'What if I fall in love with you and you don't love me?'" He looked at me with those stark naked eyes and said: "I already felt guilty on account of she's so young. If she really loved me, I'd feel bound."

Oh boy.

It reminded me of a couple of lines from a couple of different works.

In *Zorba the Greek*, Zorba (Anthony Quinn, if you saw the movie) is loved by an old woman who is teetering near the end of her life. She adores him and needs him. Zorba, who has agreed to marry her, says in his defense, "There is only one thing God will not forgive you and that is, if a woman asks you to come to her bed and you do not go…THAT, God will not forgive."

On the other hand, In Arthur Miller's *Death of a Salesman* the mother says to her two sons, Biff and Willie, "Sons, never be afraid to disappoint a woman."

I thought of enlightening Ron with these pearls of wisdom, but since they countered each other, it seemed pointless.

Ron says, "I know how stupid this seems to be. Old guys like me…."

"Watch that, Ron," I said. "You're putting our friendship in jeopardy again."

Ron looked hangdog. "Sorry."

"Okay, go on."

He wasn't looking at me. He was looking down into his vodka. "Right now I don't trust myself. I'm like a kid who just got out of high school." He glanced at me, the eyes so naked it was embarrassing for me to look at him. "Maybe junior high school. I've been protected from the real world for a long time. Especially from the world of women." He paused for a few moments, contemplating his vodka, and then looked up at me again. "You're older than me, Richard. You've had more experience. I need your help."

"Ron. You don't need any help from someone who's never had a relationship with a woman that lasted over seven years. I don't know jack, Ron. You're asking a blind man to guide you."

"Okay, okay," he says. "But you're an old timer in Cusco...."

"Watch it."

"Sorry. What I meant to say was, you know more about the folkways and mores here than I do."

"Folkways and mores." I love Ron for that. He hadn't forgotten Anthropology one oh one. However, I hardly cared to be put in the position of advisor. There's only confusion and antagonism there. But I didn't tell him that. I just said, "Okay."

"Thanks," said Ron. "I won't hold you responsible for anything. I just need a friend... an experienced friend, to talk to."

"Ron, try to look back... way back even before you were married. Do you remember the 'Southern Belle' mode?"

His heretofore naked eyes slipped into some underwear. "Ooooh, yeah," he says.

"Here, it's in spades. These girls are specialists. The more macho the men in a society, the more manipulative the women. Protection... Self preservation."

"Hunh!" said Ron, and it seemed to me his eyes pulled on a pair of pants.

But I should have known. Wisdom gained in lucid moments is atomized in the presence of the primal urge.

The next time I saw Ron, he was shaking his head in sorrow. "These people have such a hard time," he said. "I met her mother." He paused for a goodly swallow of his vodka, then threw out an aside. "She's about ten years younger than me and a good looking woman for her age."

For her age! I stifled a guffaw and let that one pass.

He screwed up his mouth, then went on. "Her husband left her a long time ago. She has to take in laundry. They don't have hot water." He pounded on the bar for emphasis. "They don't even have a goddam *refrigerator*." He lowered his head in sorrow.

Oh Boy.

I ask him, "How many live together in this broken family Ron? Or is it just the mother and the daughter?"

He looked up at me with those two big wrinkles, the vertical ones between the eyes, like he didn't understand what I was saying. He came back slowly. "There's an older sister and a two-year-old niece. Her sister's daughter. The father's working in Lima."

The "niece" part was all too familiar. I was pretty sure the "niece" was Friné's daughter. I couldn't even look Ron in the eye.

"I want to help them," he said. "I've made a lot of money and I don't need it all for myself and my kids. I can think of it as tithing."

"That's an admirable sentiment, Ron. So you're going to make a project of this family?"

For a long time he said nothing. Then finally, without looking at me, he said, "I'm in love."

Believe me, I love love as much as the next guy...maybe more, considering my absurd past. So I got right in there and played it out. "That's great Ron!" I slapped him on the back. "Who would ever have thought it from an old feller like you?" The "old feller" thing had become an acceptable joke between us. Like Richard Pryor using the "N" word.

But in the back of my mind was that two-year-old "niece."

"Have you, er, ah, shown her your room yet?"

"Not yet. I get the feeling that these people like to go slow." Then, as if to change the subject, he pulled out a little package. "I got this for her. Do you think she'll like it?" It was a necklace of silver and jade that he had bought at one of the new upscale jewelry shops in town.

"She'll love it, Ron."

His financial condition was getting about as naked as his eyes.

"I'm going to tell her how I feel tonight."

"How do you feel?"

"I told you already. I'm in love."

"How does she feel?"

"I think she feels the same way. But she hasn't said anything yet. I think she's trying to protect herself. Remember what I told you she said: 'What if I fall in love with you and you don't love me?'."

I thought about that for a while, marveling at the clever-ness of those words. This girl may be young, but she was in possession of some ancient woman ways.

The necklace must have been effective in at least one way. Two days later I saw Ron in the bar in the afternoon. It was an uncharacteristic time for him to be there.

Ron was drunk and talkative. At his request, we sat at a corner table that was sort of private. Ron absolutely had to talk to me.

"We finally did it," he said.

I like that "did it." It hearkened back to my youth. "And?"

"Well there's the thing about viagra. I was always taking it on the chance we might do it. You never know what a woman's feeling. She can seem all ready and then bring things to a screeching halt at third base. It's been a while for me and I'm not very sure of myself. I had already used up my supply of viagra on dry runs when we finally did it."

"How'd it go."

"I didn't need the stuff."

"The sex?"

"The viagra." He burst into boisterous laughter.

*   *   *   *

For days Ron was not to be seen in the bar. I imagined him in a bed of roses with Friné, screwing his brains out day and night. I was happy for him. But it wasn't as I had imagined. Ron had quietly left town without a word.

A few weeks later I got an email message from him.

Hi Richard,

Sorry to leave without saying goodbye. I got a bad shock from Friné the day after the last time you and I saw each other. Actually, the shock didn't come from Friné, it came from her mother. When I went to their house, Friné wasn't there. Her mother, Adelle, asked me in and sat me down on the sofa and told me what had happened. It turned out that the niece wasn't a niece after all. It was Friné's baby and the "brother-in-law" working in Lima was the father. Friné had taken the baby and gone to Lima to get married.

I felt like I had been hit in the stomach with a baseball bat. I'm afraid I cried. Right there in front of Adelle. I was too embarrassed to face anyone. I just ran away. I'm back home in High Point now. I'm selling my house. In spite of everything, I want to come back to Cusco. I want to live there.

See you in a few weeks.

Ron.

That seemed strange. After all that heartbreak, why would he sell his house and come back to Cusco to live?

It was more like two months before I saw Ron again. He called me on my cell phone and asked to meet me in front of the Cathedral in the Plaza. I got there early and sat on the topmost of the steps, waiting and warding off postcard vendors and shoe-shine boys. He appeared almost exactly on time. He bounded up the steps, all smiles, and threw his arms around me.

"When did you get back?"

"Three weeks ago. Have you got some time to spare? I want you to meet somebody. Then you'll understand why I haven't called you sooner."

We walked up the street of Suecia up the hill of San Cristobal until we came to a door that was newly painted. Ron pulled a key out of his pocket and unlocked the door. We entered a patio that looked like something out of a Cusco *House and Gardens*, if any such thing ever existed. All was fresh paint, flowers, grass and new lawn furniture.

Bewildered, I started to speak, "Ron, what the..."

But Ron interrupted me with a very old cliché, calling out. "Honey, I'm home!"

A pretty woman who appeared to be around forty came out into the patio. Ron embraced her and then turned to me. "This is Adelle," he said. "We're going to get married one of these days. Come on in and look at the house. There's even a *refrigerator* here now. And please stay for dinner. Adelle's teaching me local cuisine."

"*Cuy*?" I said, referring to the popular Andean dish. "Guinea pig?"

"Not yet," he said. "But probably soon."

Adelle went ahead of us into the house. She had a girlish walk and a very nice figure.

Ron watched her with undisguised admiration. When she was out of earshot he turned to me and whispered, "She's a lot more like Helen than her daughter was."

Then Old Ron shot me a sly wink to make sure I got his meaning. He took a deep breath, exhaled with satisfaction, looked around his domain with a big grin all over his face and said, "Come on in, Old pal."

THE THINGS I LOST

Why on earth would anyone want to write a piece that makes himself look stupid, foolish, senile? The answer to that question will be revealed shortly. Don't look ahead. Follow my pain to the end. It will be worth it, I promise. I am writing this last chapter because I want this to be a feel-good book.

These are some of the things I have lost in Peru. There are others, but either they are too embarrassing to relate or I have conveniently forgotten them.

The first thing I lost was in 1975. It was my first trip to Peru. It was my first day in Cusco. I was so foggy from the altitude that I lost the key to my room. I learned some of my first words in Spanish then. *He perdido me jave.* I have lost my key. I never found the key, but they gave me another and taught me a few Spanish words. For this loss, I blame altitude.

A few years later I lost a 16-millimeter Bolex movie camera with a zoom lens and a Halliburton aluminum case with custom cut foam to cradle this wonderful piece of machinery. Actually, I didn't loose it. It was stolen. But it might as well have been a loss for all the effort I made to secure it. I left it sitting on the back seat of a rented Volkswagen, shining there like silver, while I walked a beachside park in Lima. The car was locked. The walk took a bare twenty minutes, but the thieves only needed five. I chalk that one up to naivety.

Lately, I've been on a big-time stuff-losing streak. Especially, I've lost cellular telephones. A few months ago I decided that I needed to be more accessible. I don't know why. Anyone who knows me knows that they can find me in certain pubs at certain times of day. Maybe I just wanted to be cool and connected. After all, this is a cellular town. On the street, in bars, in cafes, in the theatre, the church, the meetings...cell phones are ubiquitous.

So I went to the BellSouth office (yes, BellSouth is in Cusco) and checked out their offers. I bought a little Nokia phone for $100. The phone was a giant leap over the two-year- old Motorola I was using in the US. People in Cusco looked at it with lips curled in disgust and distain and said, "It's so *big.*" It made me feel like a Pithecanthropus Erectus. So I was glad to pay the hundred just to get a cooler phone, one that wasn't so big as to put such a strain on my jean pockets. But moreover, the deal included one hundred minutes of free local calls in the first year. Incoming calls were free. After your hundred calls, the cost of a call went up to 60 cents, (US) per minute. So I was miserly with my outgoing calls. After all, I could go to a pay phone and make a local call for 14 cents (US). I wanted to save the outgoing calls for emergencies. Who knows what might happen? There are those times when one can miss a monumentally life-changing connection. Many a slip twixt the cup and the lip. Many a boogeyman out there to spoil your future. It could be the quarter you can't find to put in the parking meter. It could be a misunderstanding between PM & AM. It could be because you're aurally dyslexic and hear "rear" when they said "near" or even "tear."

I bought a little case for my new phone.. The case had a clip that attached to my belt. The clip was so tight that it was a struggle to get it onto my belt. It turned out it was easier to *remove* the case from my belt than it was to attach it.

Now here's the really embarrassing part. I hate to admit it, but I've had this experience before.... more than once. This is what happens: I look at a situation and tell myself that an accident is lurking there. I tell myself that I must do something to prevent that accident. I prevaricate, I dither and stall. It's your basic Damoclean Sword situation. It was that way with my cellular phone. The clip-on case kept falling off. It would fall off in the street and kindly citizens would pick it up and hand it to me. And I would tell myself that I needed to take this risk into account and do something about it. But before I got around to doing something about it, a group of us went to Ukuku's to dance. Oh, did I have a fine time. I danced my heart out. I was on fire. Imagine Michael Jackson with a peg leg.

I got home that night and collapsed into my bed without removing my socks. The next morning I realized that my cell phone was not with me. I thought for a while and figured out that I must have lost it at Ukukus. I went back that afternoon and was told that no one had turned it in.

My hundred-dollar phone was down the drain. Not only the phone, but all those free calls I had been saving for emergen-cies. It's the curse of a depression baby. My first move was to call my number so that I could tell the kind retriever where to return it. I called several times, but got no answers. I begin to think that maybe it was just lying in a gutter somewhere, sent to cellular oblivion by one of those taxis that is always trying to run *me* down. Maybe someone honest had found it and would return it to Ukukus, or maybe call one of the programmed numbers to find out where I am, so it can be returned..

Yah.

One day my friend Yheni, whose phone number was programmed into my lost phone, called me and played a mess-age that had been recorded on her voice mail. The message started with about two minutes of incoherent sounds, sort of rhythmic, sort of syncopated, sort of weird. And then, finally the words, whispered low and venomously, *"You'll never get it back."*

Well, that seemed pretty straightforward. I gave up on retrieving my phone along with my Cusco telephone number, my worldwide contact, the way people at home could find me in emergencies, *my connection,* you understand. I resolved to buy another. So I went back to the BellSouth office. I sat on the waiting seats that are much like airport seats only a little softer, waited while two BellSouth male service associates dealt with clients. I was feeling pretty silly already, coming here to admit that, much to my shame, I had lost a phone. The longer I had to sit there the sillier, the stupider I felt. Finally I was summoned by one of the service associates. Trying not to sound too sheepish, I told him that I had lost my cell phone.

"Que Lastima!" he says. Translate that as "Oh, too bad," or "Tough Shit," as you wish. Considering that BellSouth was about to collect another hundred bucks from me, I would suspect, "tough shit."

But I liked this guy. He was sitting tall. He was dressed in a suit. He had a nice smile. He was alert and friendly. He was one of the up and coming middle class of Cusco. Or maybe he was the boss's son. But probably not. He was too earnest to be the boss's son. He gave me the green application paper to fill in.

When I'm finished, the Bell South Associate looks at my application and lights up. It so happens he is a close friend with the family that own and run the Amaru Hostal. He stands up and shakes my hand again. He tells me that his friends call him Pocho.

I got my phone.

This time I did not buy another clip-on belt case. This time, I figured, I would keep the phone in my backpack, which is almost always with me and carries also my computer, my digital camera and assorted unmentionables, none of which I have lost. This should secure the slippery phone. But it didn't work that way. Three days later it slithered out of my bag in a taxi. I had neglected to zip up its compartment.

Now I'm really in a quandary. Maybe God didn't mean for me to have a cellular telephone. It's a sign, maybe. Besides that, can I possibly endure the embarrassment of facing Pocho again? He'll think I'm an idiot.

I wait a while, partly because of the philosophical in-decision, and partly because I figure the longer I wait to get another phone, the less foolish I will feel. Losing a phone three days after it was bought to replace your earlier lost phone is either extremely weird or a sign of *non-compus mentis*. I finally decide to go for it. I crawl sheepishly back into the BellSouth office and sit on the airport-like seats, shoulders hunched in contrition, awaiting my turn.

When I am called up to face Pocho again, I shrug with an expression of deep embarrassment.

But Pocho is gracious. He gives me an understanding look, a sympathetic look that carries not a whiff of glee. We go through the same drill with the questionnaire. I fork over ano-ther hundred, and I acquire my second phone with a new hundred minutes of free calls. This year I will not be so parsimonious with my outgoing phone calls. I think of all those precious free minutes being used by some evil thief, and I decide to *live now*. I will use up my free minutes before I lose this phone, this third phone, this embarrassment I carry with me.

This time I solved the problem... I think. I found a belt case that was not the clip-on type. This case you threaded through your belt. No amount of dancing with wild abandon could dislodge this phone. I could dance and ride in taxis and my phone would still be with me. To this day, I have this phone *and it's number* with me. Makes me proud.

I lost my electronic translator three times. My electronic translator is priceless to me. Since I refuse to go back to school, it is my primary Spanish language-learning tool. The first time I lost it was when I left it in a Taxi that was taking me to Ollan-taytambo. A very professional, very fast driver named Roberto was in command. Roberto claimed that he cold make it from the Cusco airport to Ollantaytambo in one hour and fifteen minutes. The way he drove, I could believe it. He was a fierce driver, but he was good. He was so good that I can attribute this one to awe. I managed to leave my translator in his cab.

Roberto had given me his card. I called him, but I had faint hopes. Turned out, Roberto had my translator. We made arrangements for its return. Roberto met me at Rosie's. I gave him a reward of about a third of what I paid for the thing.

The next time I left it on a combi in Ollantaytambo. Washing-ton was with me that. time. He ran after the bus like a madman and retrieved the translator.

I don't know what happened the last time. It was a terminal loss. It never came back.

I lost my glasses. I thought I had lost them that time I somersaulted down the hill below the Kachiquata quarry and banged my head on the rock. When I got back to reality I couldn't find them. Washi offered to go back to find them. No, I said, I have another pair. It turned out that the glasses were safe and secure in my inside coat pocket.

I bought a new pair of glasses in the US, but I continued to wear the old pair. I hate to surrender to weakening eyes. I perform eye exercises, but they are so boring that I'm not as good about it as I should be. After a while the frames of the old glasses broke. It's cheap to have your broken frames repaired in Cusco. Two or three dollars, maybe. I had them repaired three times. By then, spikes of solder were digging into my nose. Finally, on the fourth break, I gave up on the old glasses and took up the new. But it was not meant to be. On a New Year's Eve, I was dancing with some wild woman from Bolivia, throwing such caution to the wind that the Rosie's staff clucked tongues at me when I next resurfaced. I had the glasses hanging on my shirt and they went the way of the clip-on cellular phone. I dug out my old broken glasses and took them to my friend Dorian, my drinking buddy and optician, and asked him to put my old lenses into a new frame. That makes eight years I've been using these lenses.

I lost my "Annapolis" cap. I left it in Glenn's monster truck en route to La Paz. It was the cap I usually wore in Cusco and it reminded me that I like sailing almost as much as I love Cusco. I also lost my "Cusco" cap, which I wore in Annapolis and which reminded me that I liked Cusco even more than sailing.

I've lost all kinds of money, never to thieves, but by ignoring Polonius' advice: "Neither a borrower nor a lender be." A few people paid me back. Flaco and Popcorn boy did, but not too many others. I keep vowing never to lend money to anybody again. But I'm a sucker. My middle name, in case you've forgotten, is "just fell off the turnip truck."

I hope, dear readers, in light of this partial listing of my moronic losses, those of you who occasionally lose things, feel better about yourselves.

And those of you who never lose anything, feel smug and superior,

Hopefully, making this a feel-good book.

You probably think I'm going to end this catalogue of losses by saying that I left my heart in Cusco. Not only would that be insufferably trite, it is no so. My heart is still with me, pumping away there in its cage with the joy, and sometimes the pain, of life.

And very soon it will return with me to that place I do so much love.

The Navel of the World.